The Return of the Absent Father

Divinations: Rereading Late Ancient Religion

SERIES EDITORS:
Daniel Boyarin, Virginia Burrus, Derek Krueger

A complete list of books in the series is available from the publisher.

Haim Weiss
and Shira Stav

Translated by Batya Stein

The Return of the Absent Father

A New Reading of a Chain of Stories from the Babylonian Talmud

PENN

University of Pennsylvania Press
Philadelphia

Published by
University of Pennsylvania Press
Philadelphia, Pennsylvania 19104-4112

www.upenn.edu/pennpress

Printed in the United States of America on acid-free paper
10 9 8 7 6 5 4 3 2 1

Hardcover ISBN: 978-0-8122-5363-4
eBook ISBN: 978-0-8122-9824-6

Library of Congress Cataloging-in-Publication Data

Names: Weiss, Haim, author. | Stav, Shira, author. | Stein, Batya, translator.
Title: The return of the absent father : a new reading of a chain of stories from the Babylonian Talmud / Haim Weiss and Shira Stav ; translated by Batya Stein.
Other titles: Shuvo shel ha-av ha-ne'edar. English | Divinations.
Description: 1st edition. | Philadelphia : University of Pennsylvania Press, [2022] | Series: Divinations: rereading late ancient religion | Originally published as: Shuvo shel ha-av ha-ne'edar : ḳeri'ah meḥudeshet be-sidrat sipurim min ha-Talmud ha-Bavli (Bialik Institute, Jerusalem, 2018). | Includes bibliographical references and index.
Identifiers: LCCN 2021031890 | ISBN 978-0-8122-5363-4 (hardcover)
Subjects: LCSH: Talmud. Ketubbot V—Criticism, Narrative.
Classification: LCC BM506.K43 W4513 2022 | DDC 296.1/2—dc23
LC record available at https://lccn.loc.gov/2021031890

CONTENTS

PREFACE

A chain of seven stories in tractate Ketubot in the Babylonian Talmud centers on a narrative construct spanning two ostensibly contradictory locations: the study house (*beth midrash*) and the family. The *beth midrash*—a place for study, discussion, learning, and thought, devoted to spiritual development and to the fulfillment of intellectual yearnings—is contrasted with the family home—a place for chores, sustenance, procreation, and child-rearing. In these stories the scholar or "the sage" abandons his home, his wife, and his family and goes away to the study house for long periods lasting between a few weeks and many years. The stories revolve around moments of separation and return—dramatic moments marking the climax of the tensions between the locations representing two sides of the sage's life: his life as a scholar yearning for Torah and his life as a family man who is not actively and continuously present in the lives of the family members he left behind.

Numerous readings of this chain of stories feature in the research and interpretation of rabbinic literature. Yona Fraenkel,

Daniel Boyarin, Tal Ilan, Shulamit Valler, and Jeffrey Rubenstein have repeatedly read these stories as illustrations of the conflict between opposite values—between the value of learning, which requires a prolonged stay in the study house, and the duty to realize the value of marital life.[1] As the cycle of stories is read as thematizing the struggle between these two values, it is also read as representing a conflict between opposite desires—the desire for the woman as opposed to the desire for the Torah.

Our reason for entering this crowded scholarly area was the limited concern of these readings with the standing and function of the father. The father is a recurring character in these stories, although his shape changes from story to story and his locations vary: At times he is the actual scholar missing from the life of his children, who remained behind with their mother; at times he is the father of a groom demanding that his son go away to study Torah before consummating his marriage, and at times he is the father of the bride who functions as a kind of "third wheel"—blocking or supporting his daughter's marriage to a scholar. In our view, a slight change of focus, shifting from the tension between learning and conjugal life to the tension between fatherly presence and fatherly absence, could shed light on additional aspects that have not yet received sufficient attention: the very tension between Torah study and family life (not only conjugal intimacy), the female characters (wives and daughters) populating these stories, and the father's character in rabbinic stories in general. For us, the title *The Return of the Absent Father* touches not only on the character of the scholar who returns home to meet his children but also, and mainly, on our will to bring back the father—who is missing from the discourse that was created around this chain of stories—to the center of the discussion.

The various locations of the father in the chain of stories attest that the father's figure should be interpreted along an absence-presence axis. At one end of it is a father who is missing from his children's lives and had no part in their education and upbringing, and at the other, a father who closely supervises the lives of his sons and daughters, perhaps even vicariously living through them the life of study or of conjugal sexuality that is denied to him.

The absence-presence axis highlights the main tension that has long been related to the father figure. In some senses the father is the "most present" as well as the "most absent," both regarding his cultural function and the place assigned to him in the psyche. In Sigmund Freud's theory—in the aspect touching on psychic development and in the one dealing with the development of civilization—the father is the prominent figure, the most influential, and the most present. His threatening presence, evoking castration anxiety in the son, becomes a powerful drive in the son's mental development, which leads to the Oedipal complex solution and to fitting social integration. (Alternatively, it is the same presence that, according to Freud's Oedipal model, evokes penis envy in the daughter, leading to her limited function in the social sphere and to her restriction to the home and family space.) At the same time, the father is also the most absent. In this classic view, the mother is the physical, continuous, and sensory presence in the child's life, while the father remains a vague and intangible form, in a way that encourages his elevation to the rank of a symbol. Following Freud, Jacques Lacan sets the "symbolic father" at the center of his theory as a figure that prevails far beyond its physical manifestation and is embodied in all aspects of the patriarchal system. The father comes to signify entry into the gates of culture, conveyed in the acquisition of language and in compliance with social laws—in Lacan's terms, "the Law of the Father." As such, "the Law of the Father" depends not at all on the presence of an actual father but on the way the father's function is symbolized within the language and the discourse.

Psychoanalysis shows that, despite the dominant role assigned to the father as the founder of law, social order, language, and meaning—mainly in the constitutive theories of Freud and Lacan—his importance remains fundamentally symbolic. His place as a living and active figure within the family structure—as a person attached to his children by blood bonds as well as by psychic and emotional ties, as responsible for their sustenance, education, and growth—remains abstract and hardly a subject of theoretical concern. Psychoanalysis has undergone fundamental changes, evident in the transition from Freudian approaches to theories of object relations, beginning with Melanie Klein and Donald Winnicott and up to the intersubjective approaches of contemporary psychoanalysis that have focused on the mother and the mother-child bond, further intensifying the lacuna pertinent to the father. The ascribed existence of the father as a symbol, as the central signifier of authoritative power—all the way to the representation of God as a father, "Our Father in Heaven"—has indeed strengthened and reinforced the tendency to blur him and detract from his importance as an actual figure in family life that represents not only authority, prohibitions, and control. As we look at the father as a flesh-and-blood human figure, a body with a defined outline, a character with his own longings and his own set of identifications, one who can be weak or generous, supportive or uncaring, violent or abused, noble or wicked, the father's other visage is exposed, together with his concrete potential significance—not only the symbolic or "archetypal" one, in Carl Jung's terms—for the lives of his sons and daughters.

Although rabbinic literature, including the chain of stories we will examine, does not ignore the symbolic-theological layer, it does present a broader spectrum of father figures in various functions—distant and involved fathers, present and absent, leaving the domestic space and the concrete relationships with family members and returning to them. These diverse representations enable us to examine the father in a way that transcends the traditional ways of reading him, thereby enriching the discussion about the chain of stories, expanding it beyond the concern with the characteristic tension between the desire for learning and the desire for a partner.[2]

We see the chain of stories we will be discussing as a complete textual-talmudic set that attests, as we will try to show, to the precision and sensitivity of the editing and to the rich and complex inner dialogue that emerges between its various units.[3] Nevertheless, in Dina Stein's wake, we seek to draw a distinction between the intention of the (actual or imagined) editor and the final edited product. The question of the editor's (or the narrator's) intention when choosing these seven stories for the halakhic explication of the sages' absence from their homes is not at the center of our attention. Indeed, as Stein noted, any attempt to give real answers to this question is doomed to fail: "Subordinating the meaning of a text to its author's or editors presumed (or even professed) intention falls into the category of 'intentional fallacy.' The meaning of a text cannot be confined to the intention one attributes to the speaker/writer; the Bavli is no exception."[4] Our discussion will focus on the way the final narrative setting, including the explicit and implicit associations between its units, exposes a full assortment of metaphors, hopes, anxieties, and fears touching on the tension between the "home" and the absent "father" found at the study house, and to the influence of this absence on the complexity of the relationships between fathers and their wives, daughters, and sons. And yet the complexity of the editor's role vis-à-vis these texts cannot be ignored. The lack of clarity as to the considerations that guided the editorial choices in some sense resonates in other absences that have a bearing on this chain of stories. Like the *Deus absconditus,* and like the absent father, the editor's power lies precisely in the hidden stance he adopts and in his seeming concealment, which invite and awaken the interpretive impulse.

We ascribe to this chain of stories, using a term coined by Itay Marienberg-Milikowsky, a kind of "dynamic closure,"[5] referring to a possibility of looking at a text, so he claims, as "a maximalist reading of the story per se alongside a maximalist reading of its context and, mainly, *playing both readings, as it were, against one another.*"[6] Despite the difference between his topic (repeated stories in the Babylonian Talmud) and ours (one defined and closed chain of stories), his basic assumption about the context of the individual story appears to be valid for our reading of the current chain of stories as well. On the one hand, we propose an approach that seeks to convey the power and coherence of each separate story as well as the editorial complexity of the entire group of stories. On the other hand, we propose a reading that, rather than confining the group of stories within its own limits, seeks to acknowledge the importance of the dialogue created with its close and distant contexts—that is, its ties to both the halakhic issue it is embedded in and to other literary and halakhic rabbinic units.[7] Following Galit Hasan-Rokem, whose work on rabbinic literature rests on a claim about the heterogeneous and multivocal sources of this literature, we will also emphasize the multilayered quality of the chain of stories before us.[8] Hence, we will conduct our reading in light of literary, cultural, psychological, and folkloristic theories that emphasize the explicit and implicit dialogical quality of every text with its immediate and faraway surroundings.

This book is the product of an encounter and a dialogue between two researchers specializing in different fields of Hebrew literature. Haim Weiss is a scholar of rabbinic literature who deals with the charged sphere created through the encounter of history, literature, and folk culture and its place in modern Hebrew literature. Shira Stav studies modern Hebrew literature from a feminist and psychoanalytic perspective, with a critical emphasis on Oedipal and family structures. We wrote the book together in the belief that our combined perspectives on the texts, which rest on our different fields of research and interest, can offer new interpretations of this interesting narrative sequence and shed light on aspects that have not yet been studied.

It is an honor and a pleasure for us to thank dear colleagues and friends who were partners to the voyage. Mira Balberg, Galit Hasan-Rokem, and Dina Stein read the manuscript at various stages, commented, and helped with insights and wise suggestions. Thanks to Ruth Kara-Ivanov Kaniel, Uriah Kfir, Itamar Luria, Itay Marienberg-Milikowsky, Yaakov Tzvi Meir, Dana Olmert, and Dudu Rotman, who read the Hebrew version of the book and assisted us greatly with illuminating comments toward the writing of the English version. Special thanks to Dan Miron, who edited the Hebrew version, to Yigal Schwartz for his caring and generous accompaniment, and to Haim Be'er, lover of rabbinic literature, whose learning is embedded in the book. We are very grateful to Daniel Boyarin, editor of the series *Divinations: Rereading Late Ancient Religion*, and to the staff of the University of Pennsylvania Press, and above all to our editor, Jerry Singerman. Our unreserved appreciation goes to Batya Stein, the translator of the book, for the fine English version before you.

We are grateful to our colleagues and students in the Department of Hebrew Literature at Ben-Gurion University of the Negev for the scholarly, pleasant, and supportive surroundings, where it has been our good fortune to work and teach.

The translation of the book was made possible thanks to the kind support of Heksherim Research Institute for Jewish and Israeli Literature and Culture, the Dean of Humanities and Social Studies, and the Vice President for Research and Development at Ben-Gurion University of the Negev.

THE CHAIN OF STORIES

BT Ketubot 62b–63a

1

Thus it was with Rav Rehumi, who studied with Rava in Mahuza

and used to return home on the eve of every Yom Kippur.

Once, he was engrossed in the issue he was studying.[1]

His wife awaited him—"He's coming now, he's coming now."

He did not come.

She grew weak, and a tear fell from her eye.

At that time, he [Rav Rehumi] had been sitting on the roof. The roof collapsed under him, and he died.

2

Judah, the son of R. Hiyah, was the son-in-law of R. Yannai.

He stayed and studied at the rabbi's house and would return home every Sabbath eve. As he arrived home, he [R. Yannai] would see a pillar of fire before him.[2]

One day, he [Judah] was engrossed in the issue he was studying.

Since he [R. Yannai] did not see that sign, he said to them: "Lower his bed, for had Judah been alive, he would not have neglected the performance of his conjugal duties."

This was "as an error proceeding from the ruler," (Eccl. 10:5) and he [Judah] died.

3

Rabbi was engaged in arrangements for his son's marriage into the family of R. Hiyah.

When he was about to write the *ketubah*, the bride died.[3]

Said Rabbi, "Is there, God forbid, any flaw?"

They sat and studied [the genealogy of] the families: Rabbi was descended from Shephatyah, son of Avital, and R. Hiyah was descended from Shimei, David's brother.[4]

He [then] sought to marry his son into the family of R. Jose b. Zimra.

They agreed that he [Rabbi's son] should spend twelve years studying.

The girl was passed before him.

He said to them, "Let it be six years."

They passed her before him [again].

Said he to them, "I will marry her, and then I will go."

He felt ashamed in front of his father.

He said to him, "My son, the wisdom of your Creator is in you. It is written first, 'Thou wilt bring them in, and plant them,' (Exod. 16:17) and at the end it is written, 'And let them make me a sanctuary, that I may dwell in their midst.' (Exod. 25:8)"

He left and spent twelve years studying.

By the time he returned, his wife had become barren.

"What shall we do?" said Rabbi. "If we divorce her, it will be said—the poor soul waited in vain. If he marries yet another woman, it will be said, this one is his wife and that one his whore."

He asked for mercy for her, and she was healed.

4

R. Hanania b. Hakhinai left for the rabbi's house as the wedding feast of R. Shimon b. Yohai was coming to an end.

Said he [R. Shimon], "Wait for me, and I will come with you."

He did not wait for him.

He left and spent twelve years at the rabbi's house. By the time he returned, city streets had changed, and he knew not how to reach his house.

He went and sat by the river, where he heard voices calling to a girl, "Daughter of Hakhinai, daughter of Hakhinai, fill up your jar and let us go."

He said, "Then this is our girl," and he followed her.

His wife was sitting sifting flour. She lifted up her eyes, and as she saw him, her heart leaped, and her spirit fled.

Said he, "Lord of the universe, this poor soul—is this her reward?"

He prayed for mercy to be shown to her, and she came back to life.

5

R. Hama bar Bisa went away and spent twelve years at the study house.

When he returned [home], he said, "I will not do what Ben Hakhinai did."

He went to the study house and sent word to his home.

R. Oshayah, his son, came in and sat before him. He asked him questions on the study topics and saw that his answers [R. Oshayah's] were wise.

He was dismayed and said, "Had I been here, I would have had such a child."[5]

He entered his home, his son entered.

He [R. Hama bar Bisa] rose before him, thinking he had come to ask him a question.

His wife said to him, "Is there a father who stands up before his son?"[6]

Rami bar Hama said about him, "A threefold cord is not quickly broken" (Eccl. 4:12)—this is R. Oshayah, son of R. Hama, son of Bisa.

6

R. Akiva was a shepherd of Ben Kalba Savu'a.

His daughter, who saw that Akiva was modest and upright, said to him: "If I betroth myself to you, will you go to the rabbi's house?"

Said he, "Yes."

She was betrothed to him in secret and sent him away.

Her father heard of this, drove her away from his house, and vowed to disinherit her.

R. Akiva went away and spent twelve years at the rabbi's house.

When he returned [home], twelve thousand disciples came with him.

He heard an old man[7] saying to her, "Till when will you lead a life of living widowhood?"

Said she, "Were I the one he listens to, he would go away to study for another twelve years."

Said he [R. Akiva]: "I act with her consent."

He left again and spent another twelve years at the rabbi's house.

When he returned, twenty-four thousand disciples came with him.

His wife heard [of his arrival] and went out to meet him.

Her neighbors said to her, "Borrow some clothes to wear."

She replied: "A righteous man knows the soul of his beast." (Prov. 12:10)

On approaching him, she fell on her face and kissed his feet.

His attendants pushed her aside.

He said to them, "Leave her, mine and yours are hers."

Her father heard that a great man had come to town and said, "I shall go to him, perhaps he will release me from my vow."

He came before him.

He [R. Akiva] asked, "Would you have made your vow had you known that he would be a great man?"

Said he, "[I would not if he had known] even one chapter or even one single *halakhah*."

Said he, "I am the man."

He fell on his face, kissed his feet, and gave him half of his wealth.

R. Akiva's daughter did the same to Ben Azzai.

And on this people say, "Ewe follows ewe—like mother, like daughter."

7

Rav Yosef, the son of Rava, was sent by his father to the rabbi's house to study with Rav Yosef.

They agreed on six years for him.

After three years and with the eve of Yom Kippur approaching, he said, "I will go and see my family."

His father heard about it, took up a tool,[8] and went out to meet him.[9]

Said he [the father], "Was it your whore [*zonatkha*] you remembered?" Some say that he said, "Was it your dove [*yonatkha*] you remembered?"

They quarreled, and neither one of them ate the last meal before the fast.

INTRODUCTION

"Had I Been Here, I Would Have Had Such a Child"

When we approach the shaping of the father figure in rabbinic literature, we confront a significant absence. Stories, and even more so studies dealing directly with the father—with his concrete paternal function as the head of the family, charged with the safety, livelihood, education, and upbringing of his children and family members—are few and far between.

The limited concern with the father's place in the home and the day-to-day sphere is not unique to the rabbinic period, and we certainly do not view this as evidence of this figure's ostensible unimportance. The opposite is true: Precisely the lack of attention to the father's function within the family sphere (as opposed to the extensive concern with him as a major agent in the cultural sphere) and to his role as a vital and cardinal figure in the education and development of his children—both sons and daughters—is what attests to the traditional perception of paternal power as unquestionably "obvious," seemingly not in need of comment. As Ursula Owen notes, within the domestic sphere of the patriarchal family, bringing up children and caring for them is almost exclusively the mother's role. She is identified with the house, with the inside, with the family, while the father is perceived as almost the sole link to the world outside.[1] Women in rabbinic literature who, in Galit Hasan-Rokem's definition, are "reflections of male images of women and projections of male expectations from them," are naturally located in a sphere that men seek to avoid: the home and its day-to-day tiresome and exhausting routine.[2] The father seeks to be the sole representative of the life of culture, spirit, and knowledge. In its realization, Torah study is obviously a central category in the rabbinic world, except that this life remains outside the home.[3] The way the father actualizes his paternal role within the domestic realm—in the hourly and daily routine that is identified mostly with the woman—remains, as it were, unknown.[4]

Through a new look at the chain of stories in tractate Ketubot, we wish to place at the center of our discussion that very "obviousness" of the father's high hierarchical position within the family, ponder it, describe it, and highlight the tensions entailed by it. This chain of stories examines the relationships between the home and the study house, but in our view, as noted, it is no less an examination of the father's standing and function in his home vis-à-vis his wife and mainly vis-à-vis his sons and daughters. In these stories the study house, a realm competing with and opposed to the family, is a locus that enables the discussion of the father's figure (or, at times, the figure of the son or the son-in-law) along the absence-presence axis. The absence and presence concepts kindle the issue of the father's standing, power, and authority, which can no longer be viewed as obvious.

This literary complex, as mentioned, has received extensive scholarly attention and has been a subject of detailed analyses by Yona Fraenkel, Daniel Boyarin, Shulamit Valler, Tal Ilan, and

Jeffrey Rubinstein.[5] Despite the significant differences in their hermeneutical positions, all these authors describe a realm centered on the conjugal relationship, relating to the influence of the husband's absence mainly on his relationship with his wife.[6] In their view, the central tension manifest in various ways in this narrative sequence is that between the allure of Torah study and the passion it evokes on the one hand, and, on the other, the husband's sexual and conjugal obligations toward his wife.[7] Their reading, emphasizing and intensifying the conjugal drama, rests mainly on the halakhic context of the narrative sequence, as defined in the Mishnah:

> If a man vowed to have no intercourse with his wife, the School of Shammai says: [She may consent] for two weeks. And the School of Hillel says: For one week [only]. Disciples [of the Sages] may continue absent for thirty days against the will [of their wives] while they occupy themselves in the study of the Law; and laborers for one week. The *duty of marriage* enjoined in the Law is: every day for them that are unoccupied; twice a week for laborers; once a week for ass-drivers; once every thirty days for camel-drivers; and once every six months for sailors. So R. Eliezer.[8]

In the Hebrew original, the man "excludes" his wife (*medir et ishto*) from intercourse. This exclusion and the perception that the wife is subject to the husband's authority are emphasized against the background of the surrounding Mishnah units. The one preceding it deals with the definition of the wife's duties toward her husband: "These are the works which the wife must perform for her husband: grinding flour and baking bread and washing clothes and cooking food and giving suck to her child and making ready his bed and working in wool." The ones that follow consider the wife's status vis-à-vis her husband as a rebellious wife: "If a woman will not consent [to marital intercourse] with her husband, he may reduce her *ketubah* by seven *denars* for every week,"[9] or as one whose husband supports her through a third person: "If a husband maintained his wife at the hands of a third person."[10] What prompted the discussion in the Mishnah is indeed the husband's obligation toward his wife to engage in regular sexual intercourse, and, seemingly, what concerns the participants in the discussion are the wife's needs.[11] And yet the power to exclude from sexuality—like the power to satisfy it—is still the husband's, and the discussion in the Mishnah focuses on the limits and scope of his power.

This exclusion from the control over sexuality parallels the obvious exclusion of women from Torah study, which is not specified in the text. This is one expression of the hidden parallel between sexual activity and Torah study as if the two were mutually exclusive since both, as it were, meet the same needs, a parallel Boyarin has also pointed out. Inseparable from this control over sexual activity (who has the power to exclude whom) is the relative freedom the Mishnah grants the husband to come and go as he wishes—a freedom largely inaccessible to the wife. The woman's place is in the home, and, in fact, she is the home's distinctive representation. At the linguistic level, she is even the home itself, as in R. Judah's saying: "His house—that is his wife."[12] In Aramaic, too, the word denoting "wife" is *devitho*, which translates literally as "of the home."[13] By contrast, the man is characterized by free movement from the home/wife to outside territories, such as foreign countries. This movement enables him to leave behind his wife and family, who are at times (in the father's name) protected by and in the charge of a guardian whose substitute presence emphasizes the huge absence of the husband and father.

A story from Leviticus Rabba illustrates well the huge anomaly of a woman's free movement, out of her home and back, particularly when related to the experience of study and the passion for it discussed in the chain of stories considered here:[14]

> Rabbi Ishmael taught: "Peace is so important that a name written in holiness can be erased in the water, to make peace between a husband and his wife."
>
> Rabbi Meir used to sit and teach on the Sabbath nights.
>
> A certain woman sat there listening to him. Once his discourse went on, she waited until he had finished, went home, found the candle had died down.
>
> Her husband said to her, "Where were you?"
>
> She said to him, "I was sitting and listening to the teacher."
>
> He said, "I swear that you will not enter here until you go and spit in the face of the teacher."
>
> She stayed away the first week, two, and a third.
>
> The neighboring women said to her, "Since you are still angry with each other, we will take you with us to the teacher."
>
> When Rabbi Meir saw them, he saw the Holy Spirit. He said to them, "Is there anyone among you learned in the magical curing of eyes?"
>
> Her neighbors said to her, "Now go and spit in his face, and you will be permitted to your husband."
>
> When she sat before him, she withdrew from him.
>
> She said to him, "Rabbi, I am not learned in the magical curing of eyes."
>
> He said to her, "Spit in my face seven times, and I will be cured."
>
> She spat in his face seven times.

> He said to her, "Go tell your husband, 'You said one time, and I spat seven times.'"
>
> His disciples said to him, "Thus to dishonor the Torah? Would it not have been better to ask one of us to cure you?"
>
> Said he to them, "Is it not enough for Meir to be like his Maker? For Rabbi Ishmael taught, 'Peace is so important that a name written in holiness can be erased in the water, to make peace between a husband and his wife.'" [Leviticus Rabba 9:9][15]

This midrash tells a story about a woman whose return home on the eve of the Sabbath was delayed because she had been listening to R. Meir preaching in the synagogue. When she returned home, her husband refused to let her in until she went and spat in the preacher's face. The woman remained sitting at the door of her house for three weeks, until her neighbors took her to R. Meir. To make peace between her and her husband, R. Meir persuaded her to spit in his face seven times on the pretext that this quasi-medical, quasi-magical action would heal his eyes.[16] In many ways this story reverses in terms of gender, and thus also in terms of direction (usually from the house to the study house), the chain of stories we consider in this work. Here the wife is the one who is attracted to study and, because of it, is delayed on the eve of the Sabbath (as in the story of Rav Rehumi and his wife or that of Judah, R. Hiyah's son-in-law), while the husband is the one sitting at home waiting for her. As Hasan-Rokem notes, the story contradicts an accepted finding in ethnographic literature, whereby "the women rule in the inner spaces while the men—in the outer spaces and in the public areas."[17] The narrator, as well as R. Meir, who purportedly support the woman, see no blame in her actions and identify the violent element in the husband's demand. Ultimately, however, the resolution of the dispute attests that the aim of returning the woman to her home and to her husband overrides the open critique of the husband's actions, bearing out the effectiveness of his violent behavior. The entire story is built around the deviant behavior of the woman, who prefers studying to staying home. This deviance is emphasized in the woman's prolonged stay in the liminal space of the house's threshold, a situation that requires the enlistment of a female community—the neighbors—as well as the rabbi's help to return the deviant woman to her "right" place, as the husband perceives it, as part of the home.

This return to the domestic space is compatible with the insights of Sherry B. Ortner. She shows that, traditionally, the woman is identified with the family structure, whereas the man is identified with the public structure: The woman's biology (pregnancy, birth, and nursing) endows her, as it were, with "natural" skills for the family association, and therefore she "represents lower-level, socially fragmenting, particularistic sort of concerns, as opposed to interfamilial relations representing higher-level, integrative, universalistic sorts of concerns. . . . And hence, so the cultural reasoning seems to go, men are the 'natural' proprietors of religion, ritual, politics, and other realms of cultural thought and action in which universalistic statements of spiritual and social synthesis are made."[18] This is an almost transhistorical patriarchal structure, which is prominently present in rabbinic and in modern Western culture. As Pierre Bourdieu indicates, these are gender categories that survive beyond time and place through their ceaseless reproduction by both individual and institutional agents—from the family up to the entire society.[19] It merits mention in this context that, as Joan W. Scott shows, at any given time the definition and demarcation of "gender differences" as well as the sociocultural emergence of approaches dealing with the roles suitable for men and women function as the organizing principles in the gender balance of power, too.[20]

The mishnah we are dealing with touches on the definition of the husband's sexual duties toward his wife, and mainly on the relationship between the husband's occupation—laborer, sailor, ass driver, or student—and this duty. Of all the occupations mentioned in the Mishnah, the talmudic discussion naturally focuses on scholars and on the maximal period they are allowed to be absent from home for the purpose of studying Torah. The talmudic determination that precedes the chain of stories significantly lengthens the period of absence allowed in the Mishnah:

> For sailors, once in six months. These are the words of R. Eliezer. . . . In the name of Rav, the Halakhah follows R. Eliezer. Said R. Adda b. Ahavah in the name of Rav: This is the view of R. Eliezer, but the rabbis ruled that students go away to study Torah for two or three years without permission.
>
> BT Ketubot 62b

Immediately after the rabbis' view, Rava is cited: "The rabbis relied on R. Adda b. Ahavah and themselves acted accordingly."[21] The chain of stories discussed here is then quoted to support this claim, showing that rabbis were indeed absent from their homes for many years. In Adiel Schremer's formulation, "Many sages favored intellectual pursuits over actual married life."[22]

The halakhic context, as noted, as well as the manifest content of some of these stories, led the scholars mentioned earlier to view this narrative complex as reflecting mainly a conjugal drama. The difference between them, especially between Boyarin on the one hand and Valler and Fraenkel on the other, is in their perception of the cultural and theological meaning of the entire sequence. As will be shown in the course of the reading, Boyarin emphasizes the conjugal tensions arising from the stories, whereas Valler and Fraenkel, in what we view as an apologetic stance, try to extract a positive meaning from this narrative sequence and present it as one where sages do take into account the woman's opinions and wishes.[23]

In the reading we suggest, we will stress additional aspects of the drama, which is definitely not only conjugal and male but also a complex family dynamic that often focuses on the relationship between the father and his sons and daughters. The broad family context emphasizes the complexity of the father's absence or presence not only for his wife but also—and in some of the stories mainly—for his children.[24] Reading the chain of stories solely through the conjugal prism or through that of the tension between Torah study and sexual fulfillment misses the family drama latent in the stories and the variations in the rabbis' perception of the father's standing vis-à-vis his offspring. A reading that diverts us from the conjugal setting to the general family sphere affords a unique and interesting glimpse into the drama of the relationship between fathers and sons and even into a topic hardly ever discussed either in the rabbinic or the scholarly literature—the drama of the relationship between fathers and their daughters.

Except for the first story in the sequence, where only Rav Rehumi and his wife appear, all the six stories that follow present an encounter between children and their father whose intensity varies from one story to another. The story of Rav Rehumi, although certainly part of this narrative chain, is separated by another unit from the other six stories, which appear later in one sequence.

An examination of the six stories reveals that not only do all of them include an encounter between a father and his children but also that this chain has a kind of inner order—three stories about fathers and sons and three stories about fathers and daughters, which are presented alternately: a story about a father and a daughter followed by one about a father and a son, and so on throughout the entire sequence. Immediately after the story about Rav Rehumi and his wife is a story that describes R. Yannai supervising the relationship of his daughter with Judah. After that comes the story of R. Judah ha-Nasi searching for a suitable partner for his son. Next is the story about R. Hanania b. Hakhinai following his daughter, who does not recognize him, and then a story describing R. Hama b. Bisa teaching Torah to his son R. Oshayah. The next story opens with Ben Kalba Savu'a's ban on his daughter and ends with R. Akiva releasing him from his vow. The last story in the chain deals with Rava, who controls the norms of study and the passion of his son, Rav Yosef.

Most of these stories, except for that of Rav Rehumi, appear to involve some displacement of the relationship's focus—from the tension within the couple due to the prolonged separation to the conflict between a father and a son or a father-in-law and a son-in-law (or perhaps also between a father and God, as in the story about Hanania b. Hakhinai). Caught in the middle, between two men, are the mother and the daughters. This displacement presents an additional mode of suppressing the female voice in the stories—its marginalization or its total exclusion—when the conjugal drama between a man and a woman turns into a drama between two men. In what follows we will see this displacement and suppression occurring even more intensely when the tension between father and daughter is resolved through the relationship between father-in-law and son-in-law, as in the story of R. Yannai and Judah.

THE FIRST STORY

Rav Rehumi and His Wife

Shulamit Valler, Yona Fraenkel, Daniel Boyarin, and Jeffrey Rubenstein emphasize the strong condemnation of the practice of prolonged absences from home and the neglect of the wife's needs resonating in this story.[1] Rav Rehumi's very choice to visit his home on Yom Kippur, when sexual relations are forbidden, entails a sadistic aspect in its dismissal of the sexual and emotional relationships between the spouses. The rabbis categorically condemn this, as evident in Rav Rehumi's cruel death.[2] A warranted consequence of the rabbis' condemnation as conveyed in the text, then, is the justification of female desire and its reflection in the text. The sexuality of Rav Rehumi's wife is conveyed here through her desperate waiting, longing for her partner's arrival, and through the tear that falls from her eye—in a way a sublimation of the fluid, pervasive female desire. But despite what originally appeared as the "empathetic depiction of the eagerly waiting wife," as Boyarin sees it,[3] several issues emerging here merit attention. Not only is Rav Rehumi strongly punished, but so is his wife, who loses him altogether precisely when she yearns for him so much. In Aramaic, the *r–h–m* root also means "love," and Rav Rehumi's loss attests, above all, to the loss of love, since the woman has lost her beloved. In fact, she lost him at the moment he left to study Torah, and the temporary absence (Torah study) turned into a permanent one (death). He is indeed punished with death—but she is punished with widowhood and loses the man who is dear to her. Seemingly, both Rav Rehumi and the authorities judging him—the punishment that is meted out to him from heaven—behave similarly toward the woman and unequivocally disregard her desire, in a denial that culminates in absolute negation. Thus this story could be viewed as endorsing a positive attitude toward the woman only insofar as we deal with her not as a subject but as a component of the system preserving the family commandments. Once we move on to examine the subjective needs, wishes, and feelings expressed in the story, however, it is impossible to ignore that she is harshly punished, too.

Why must the text punish her? The woman's desire is represented here through a wondrously subtle image—the tear. In this case, desire works according to a "mechanics of fluids," to use a concept coined by Luce Irigaray: that is, as part of a "female logic" that dissolves the borders between concepts seemingly solid and rational, or phallocentric and "male." Rather than as an essentialist category of gender differences, we approach this Irigaray concept as pointing to different qualities that, within the culture, have accumulated gender significance. As Noa Walden's study shows, crying in rabbinic literature cannot be claimed to be an exclusively female experience, and rabbinic stories often describe sages who cry.[4] But the fluidity—in contrast to the solidity placed within demarcation lines defining its form—emerges here as an image of shapelessness, as something that, despite its delicacy, invariably entails a risk of gushing and flooding, breaching borders and crushing dams.

The Babylonian Talmud contains other instances of male anxiety about the power of female sorrow, a power that is conveyed in weeping beyond the limits that the halakhic discourse allows. Thus, for example, a short story in BT Mo'ed Katan directly and violently emphasizes the cultural effort to control weeping and enclose it within defined borders. The sanctions imposed for the breach of these norms, which is perceived as noncompliance with the male authority that set them, are particularly violent:

> Said Rav Judah, citing Rav, "One who grieves too much over his dead one will weep for another."
>
> That woman, who was Rav Huna's neighbor, had seven sons.
>
> One of them died, and she wept for him too much.[5]
>
> Rav Huna sent [word] to her: "Do not do that."
>
> She did not heed him.
>
> He sent [word] to her, "If you obey, it is well, and if not—make provision [a shroud] for another dead."
>
> And all died.[6]
>
> Finally, he said to her, "Make provision [a shroud] for yourself." And she died.[7]
>
> BT Mo'ed Katan 27b[8]

The story is cited in a discussion dealing with the bounds of mourning and focuses on the statement of Rav Judah in the name of Rav: "One who grieves too much over his dead one will weep for another." Rav does not define "too much." (The Gemara will do so immediately after the story.) In a cruel psychological insight, however, he claims that this is actually a way of displacing sorrow from one death to another, from a death one is now allowed to mourn to another that becomes an object of the redundant mourning. Rav Huna is not willing to allow the mourning woman to sink into her sorrow, perhaps fearing she will be engulfed by it, and views her unwillingness to abide by halakhic mourning norms as a subversive antiestablishment move that, aided by weeping and tears, seeks to resist the norm regimenting grief.[9]

Rav Huna's reaction points to his readiness to engage, at the expense of the remaining children, in a violent and cruel struggle over the ownership of grief and weeping. Rav Huna wields his halakhic magic authority to compel the woman to grieve exclusively within the bounds of Halakhah.[10] The mother, who either cannot or does not want to control the "excessiveness" of her crying, unintentionally triggers a martyrological struggle for her right to mourn, which leads to the death of all her other children.[11] Her boundless grief for the death of her firstborn detaches her from her basic role as a mother, which is to protect her children and preserve them from harm.[12] The antithetical gender positions presented in this story—a male rule controlling grief and mourning versus a female "excessiveness" that cannot (and may not even want to) abide by the regimenting norm—ultimately lead to the death of all her children and even to the death of the mourning woman herself.[13]

As in the story about the mourning mother and Rav Huna, so in the story at the focus of this chapter, the excessiveness of Rav Rehumi's wife's tear emerges as an emblem of death. The sublimation of her desire and its reduction to a tear effectively disguise the troubling and destructive, even annihilating, dimension of excessiveness, which is ascribed to her sexual feelings and to heterosexual love itself. As the tear falls—crossing the borders of the body, flooding the woman/container—Rav Rehumi falls through a gap that opened up in the roof.[14] The response to the crossing of the body's borders is the dangerous collapse of the "male" structure's stable perimeter—the *beth midrash*—and the opening of a female hole that destroys the stable spiritual structure Rav Rehumi had built for himself.[15] It is here that the symmetry between Rav Rehumi and his wife becomes clear. True, physical sexuality is represented solely by her character, whereas her husband's sexuality is entirely transformed into intellectual passion, into Torah study. Both of them, however, yielded to the passion of excessiveness, the "too much"—he, who was swept into his learning, and she, who did not prevent her tear/desire from erupting. Both are severely punished by the law and by the logic of stable borders, and this symmetry challenges the rigidity of gender differences as well. The failure to keep boundaries is evident not only in the spatial dimension—the boundaries of the body, the home, and the *beth midrash*—but also in the shaky temporal dimension where both Rav Rehumi and his wife are placed. The husband's attraction to learning blurs for him the importance of the calendar regarding the setting of dates and making time for his waiting wife. He is entirely immersed in the immediate experience of forgetting himself within the study of Torah. Similarly, his wife lacks a continuous and linear consciousness of time as proceeding from one hour to the next. The repetition of "he is coming now" places her completely in a present-time dimension, outside a chronology moving along a sequence from past to future. For both of them this flawed temporality signals a deviation from the male structures of the discourse, which insist on regular linearity, on separation, on allocations and defined realms. Worth noting in this context is Julia Kristeva's description of the time dimension in female subjectivity, a traditional perception related to the concepts of repetition and eternity:

> On the one hand, there are cycles, gestation, the eternal recurrence of a biological rhythm which conforms to that of nature

> and imposes a temporality whose stereotyping may shock, but whose regularity and unison with what is experienced as extra subjective time, cosmic time, occasion vertiginous visions and unnameable *jouissance*. On the other hand, and perhaps as a consequence, there is the massive presence of a monumental temporality, without cleavage or escape, which has so little to do with linear time (which passes) that the very word "temporality" hardly fits.[16]

Rav Rehumi is punished for his failure to keep precise boundaries, for the excess in his relationship with the object of his desire, the Torah. His name, too, implicitly conveying the word womb (*rehem*), is extremely significant: If the *beth midrash* is a womb of learning, Rehumi's sitting on the roof represents the place of his choice—a redundant location, neither positive nor fertile, outside the womb. Thus his death hints at the death of the option epitomized by the womb, and possibly also to the fate of his wife as a widow.[17]

An interesting comparison is that between the story of Rav Rehumi, who sits down to study on the roof, and the story about Hillel the Elder's beginnings as a scholar, which is also tied to the roof of the study house:

> They said about Hillel the Elder that every day he used to work and earn one tropaik—half of it he would give to the guard at the study house and half he would spend on himself and his family. One day he found nothing to earn and the guard at the study house did not allow him to enter. He climbed up and sat on the edge of a stack to hear the words of the living God from Shmaya and Avtalyon. They said: that was the eve of a Sabbath, and it was the time of Tevet

> [a winter month] and snow fell on him from heaven. When dawn rose, Shmaya said to Avtalyon: Avtalyon my brother! Every day this house is lit, and today it is dark, is it perhaps a cloudy day? They looked up and saw the figure of a man in the stack. They went up and found that he was covered by three cubits of snow. They took him down, bathed him, oiled him, placed him opposite the fire and said, "This man deserves that the Sabbath be desecrated on his behalf."
>
> BT Yoma 35b

In this story, as in the story of Rav Rehumi, the roof of the study house is a place where a person sinks into study until he loses sense of time and place. Furthermore, it also denotes a liminal point in time, the transition from an ordinary weekday to the eve of the Sabbath, when the desire for study undermines the spatial, physical, and temporal delimitations. Hillel's presence on the roof blocks access to light in the study house, his body is covered in snow and becomes an ice statue, and the Sabbath is desecrated due to the need to warm him up and nurture him back to health. Despite the similarity between the stories, however, they are actually antithetical, as evident from the opposite fates that befell Hillel and Rav Rehumi. Hillel's story is shaped as a hagiography, describing the beginning stages of an intellectual ancestor's learning, whereas Rav Rehumi's story describes his ending and death. The difference between the stories may also be ascribed to the gender gap between them: In the story of Hillel, the men sitting in the *beth midrash* are the ones who decode his radical behavior and his willingness to ignore the members of his household on the eve of the Sabbath so he can listen from the roof to the teachings of Torah sages. Thus they see his behavior as appropriate and present him as an ideal model of a sage. By contrast, the absence of Rav Rehumi is decoded by his wife.

In her view the absence emphasizes the disappearance, and therefore deconstructs the ideal dimension of his action and leads to his death. A further difference between the stories is that the story of Rav Rehumi punishes the couple for not consummating their conjugal relationship, whereas the story of Hillel replaces the husband-wife relations on the Sabbath eve with a sublimated and symbolic erotic mating between the student and the *beth midrash*, which is represented figuratively: Hillel's body, covered by three cubits of snow, turns into a (male) ice statue that covers the (female) stack hole. The story thereby hints at the advantage of the *beth midrash* as a place of desire over the home and the wife, an advantage affirmed and supported by the protective and caring (almost motherly) response of Shmaya and Avtalyon.

Let us return to our story. The narrator's focus on the tear and on the delicate description of its fall as a representation of the desire, the longings, and the frustration of Rav Rehumi's wife directs attention to other instances in the Babylonian Talmud where the act of crying focuses on the tear and on its movement from the eye of the crying person toward the world. BT Gittin has the story of "the carpenter's apprentice," the last in a sequence of legends (aggadot) about the destruction of the Temple. The story describes carnivalesque class reversals, where the rabbi turns into an apprentice and the apprentice turns into a rabbi. The dramatic culmination of the reversal is subtly and sensitively described through the fall of tears:

> Said Rav Judah, in the name of Rav: "What is meant by the verse, 'They oppress householder and house, people and their inheritance'" [Micha 2:2].[18]
>
> There was once a man who desired his master's wife, and he was a carpenter's apprentice.[19]

One day, his master needed to borrow some money.

Said he to him, "Send your wife to me, and I will lend her the money."

He sent his wife to him.

He stayed with her for three days.[20]

He then went to him and said, "Where is my wife whom I sent to you?"

He replied: "I sent her away at once, but I heard that the youngsters abused her on the way."

Said he, "What shall I do?"

He said, "If you heed my advice, divorce her."

Said he, "She has a large marriage settlement."

He said, "I will lend you money and give her settlement.

This one went and divorced her, and the other went and married her.

Since the time came for returning the loan and he could not pay back, he said, "Come and work off your debt with me."

So they would sit and eat and drink and he would wait on them, and tears would fall from his eyes and drop into their cups, and it was from that hour that the sentence was sealed [the destruction of the Temple].

BT Gittin 58a

The rabbi's master's tears and those of Rav Rehumi's wife are intriguingly similar. In both cases the reason for crying is the breakup of a couple's relationship and the breakup of their home (both as their physical dwelling and as a symbol of their mutual trust), which one of the partners, (Rav Rehumi or the wife of the apprentice's master) has abandoned to enter a new relationship (with the study house in the former case or with another man in the latter). Indeed, in both cases tears lead to the destruction of the home, and Irigaray's claim seemingly applies to both the male and female weeping. The tear of Rav Rehumi's wife leads to a personal family calamity, whereas the master's tears for the collapse of the entailed social hierarchies lead to a national calamity that culminates in the destruction of the Temple. The common lines of the two stories point to the destabilizing and crumbling power of weeping and to its signification as the poetic justice both stories strive for. But this justice is destructive: The spouses' betrayal of their loyalty to their families leads not only to the punishment of those who sinned (Rav Rehumi or the carpenter's apprentice) but also to the complete destruction of both the family and the institutional frameworks.

THE SECOND STORY

Judah, Son of R. Hiyah

This is ostensibly a story about two men, R. Yannai and Judah, but the tie between them rests on the connection to a third, hidden, figure who does not appear in the story: R. Yannai's daughter, who is Judah's wife. This hidden figure is the crux of the plot, which deals with the son-in-law's–and the father's—attraction to the daughter, and with the regimentation of this very attraction.

The exclusion of the daughter from the story is a common feature in a textual culture that leaves little room for the father-daughter relationship in the familial, social, and public spaces. Most of this culture's narratives are patriarchal: The father heads the political, religious, social, and literary hierarchy, and the narratives build transmission and legacy from father to son, thus ensuring the continuance of paternal authority. In this context rabbinic literature continues the gender norm common in biblical literature, which allocates hardly any room to female characters and to the female voice. The woman's exclusion is most evident in the dynastic sequences transmitted in the Torah, which mention only the names of fathers and sons. The mother's role in the procreation chain is never stated; she is erased, and instead the father is the one noted as having engendered the child. The daughter's place is erased, too, and, except in special cases and unusual narratives (such as, for example, the story of Dina or that of the daughters of Zelophchad), her name and her story are not mentioned.[1]

According to the anthropological studies of Claude Lévi-Strauss, "the total relationship of exchange which constitutes marriage is not established between a man and a woman, but between two groups of men, and the woman figures only as one of the objects in the exchange, not as one of the partners."[2] In this sense daughters are an asset exchanged between men in a way that enables them to preserve their power and strengthen the ties and alliances between them. Lévi-Strauss shows that the exogamy pattern (mating with women from outside the family) determines and fixes the father and daughter functions within the family: The father is the one who exchanges; the daughter is the one exchanged. Exogamy, then, as a value that conditions the cultural organization, relies, as Lynda Boose shows, on the two characters that sustain it: the father and the daughter.[3] But while the culture protects and legislates the father's status, the daughter's place is repressed and erased by being the factor made redundant by the father. Hortense Spillers shows that the legacy lines from father to daughter are consistently tortuous, and never as straight as those from father to son. Eventually, the daughter will discard her father's name, his law, and his influence for the sake of those of another man; thus she is merely a temporary component of the family. The daughter, then, is suspended between longstanding institutionalized territories: At first she bears her father's name, and then she receives a new one—that of her husband and father of her children. Her status as daughter is preserved only until she "disappears"; that is, when she collapses into the roles of wife and mother of another man's children.[4]

Consequently, status gaps between father and daughter in patriarchal families are the widest of all. Whereas the father possesses legal power and authority, the daughter is entirely deprived of them. She lacks any legal power of her own; eventually she will also leave her original nuclear family to become a mother in a new nuclear family. From the moment of her transition to the authority of another man, she disappears almost completely from her original family setting.[5]

The story in this chapter successfully illustrates this power gap, given that the daughter is never mentioned. It opens with a peaceful description of ostensible family harmony: "Judah, the son of R. Hiyah, was the son-in-law of R. Yannai. He stayed and studied at the rabbi's house and would return home every Sabbath eve." Judah would leave for his studies every Sunday and would return home to his wife every Sabbath eve. Contrary to the previous story about Rav Rehumi, as well as to the stories that follow, which describe prolonged absences from home, the absence here seems reasonable. The dissonance, however, appears already in the second sentence: "As he arrived home, he [R. Yannai] would see a pillar of fire before him." Yona Fraenkel claims that the presence of a pillar of fire "is explained by them [as representing] a holy man arriving to observe a commandment."[6] The commandment that Fraenkel refers to is obviously the conjugal obligation incumbent on the husband, with the pillar of fire representing his sexual passion. Daniel Boyarin says so explicitly: "The 'pillar of fire' is highly charged as an erotic symbol, since it is phallic in shape and since fire has strongly erotic associations."[7] Both Fraenkel and Boyarin approach the story through the central axis of the entire narrative, that is, the presence or absence of tension between Torah study and the conjugal commandment.[8] We, however, ask why the father, R. Yannai, tracks the lust of his son-in-law. The picture that emerges here is that every Sabbath eve, R. Yannai would stand and wait to see the pillar of fire heralding the arrival of his son-in-law and thus the consummation of the sexual act between Judah and his daughter. This is the gaze of a father—perhaps controlling, perhaps voyeuristic—unwilling to let his daughter lead an independent life with her husband, a life he has absolutely no share in.

The sages' awareness of the power informing this controlling and voyeuristic gaze is evident in other talmudic texts, and we will cite two of them. The first is a brief passage from BT Sanhedrin referring to an ancient source in Ben Sira:

> A daughter is a vain treasure to her father.
> Anxious for her, he does not sleep at night.
> As a child—lest she be seduced,
> as a young girl—lest she play the harlot,
> as an adult—lest she does not marry, if she marries—lest she bear no children,
> as she grows old—lest she pursues witchcraft.[9]
>
> BT Sanhedrin 100b

The father is described here as consumed by anxiety about his daughter, from her childhood up to her old age. The brief and paranoid text reveals the—mainly sexual—threat the daughter poses to her father and particularly to his power, honor, and authoritative standing in the family and in the community. In fact the threat alone is enough to weaken and daunt the father. He cannot sleep at night and ceaselessly imagines his daughter exceeding the boundaries of the controlling space: She is tempted, she is slutty, she may not get married and may not bear children, and finally, when the sexual options are no longer valid, she becomes a witch. The text exposes the fact that the father's social and communal status is affected by his daughter's behavior. The father's anxiety about his daughter's improper sexual conduct reflects his anxiety about its effect on his standing. All the fears are tied to the temporary and borderline standing of the daughter and to her existence as a liminal figure on the border between inside and outside, between her being an asset to her father and her future as an asset to another man, between her temporary status as a virgin and her mission as a mother. Hence relationships between fathers and daughters are presented in most texts—both ancient and modern—through this conceptual duality of the daughter as the weak (or, more precisely, weakened) figure in the family, and of the daughter as a threatening and subversive figure holding the power to make her father lose sleep.[10] As for R. Yannai, the impression is that his gaze at Judah, his son-in-law, goes beyond the worry detailed in Ben Sira, "having a husband, lest she should . . . become barren." Indeed, the commandment not to neglect his conjugal duty is compatible with the commandment of procreation, but something in the persistent tracking of the son-in-law and in the hasty, bleak conclusion that R. Yannai draws from Judah's tardiness attests to an active emotional involvement that is not solely limited to concern about the continuity of his progeny.

The second text dealing with a voyeuristic and controlling gaze appears in BT Ta'anit and describes the violent anxiety of R. Jose of Yokeret, which leads to his daughter's death:

> He [R. Jose of Yokeret] had a beautiful daughter.
>
> One day, he [R. Jose] saw a man who had made a hole in the fence and was looking at her.[11]
>
> Said he to him, "What is this?"

> He answered, "Master, if I am not allowed to take her, will I not be allowed to see her?" Said he, "My daughter, you bring sorrow to people; return to your dust and may they not transgress because of you."[12]
>
> BT Ta'anit 24a

In a way, this story is a concretization of the amorphous anxiety that appears in the talmudic reading of Ben Sira. The daughter of R. Jose of Yokeret is described at the opening as "beautiful." The description of a character as "beautiful," all the more so a female character, is extremely rare in rabbinic literature. As in other cases, the beauty is undefined and lacks distinct aesthetic features but is instead a kind of quality, touching more on the figure's character than on her appearance. Beauty is designed not to create an aesthetic experience in the reader but to mark a space of danger and confrontation in the plot. R. Jose of Yokeret, who supervises and controls his daughter's behavior, sees a man peeking at her through a hole in the fence surrounding the house.[13] R. Jose turns to him and asks him, "What is this?"—what is the pleasure you are experiencing, or, what pleasure do you derive from this voyeurism?[14] The man's response creates a hierarchy between several ways of fulfilling desire. At the head of the list is sexual gratification: "if I am not allowed to take her . . ." Since he cannot marry this woman, he will be satisfied with the sexual gratification derived from peeping through the fence. R. Jose understands, then, that his wish to exert total control over his daughter's sexuality by hiding her is doomed to fail, since a gap of some kind will invariably be found that will enable seeing her.

Furthermore, one can hardly ignore that the very piercing of a hole in the fence entails symbolic sexual meaning, like that of piercing and penetrating a body. R. Jose understands that the voyeuristic sexual pleasure is itself a symbolic desecration of the body/home, which is supposed to be absolutely confined within the father's realm of control.[15] Hence piercing (*nikuv*) the fence is tantamount to the feminization of the father himself (turning him into a *nekevah*), that is, a real erosion of his patriarchal power. The daughter's beauty and attractiveness could have signaled her high value in the marriage-exchange market, and thus also the value of the entire household. For R. Jose, however, her beauty turns from an asset into a vulnerability. Peeping at the beautiful daughter, publicly exposes the source of his weakness and thereby endangers the implementation of his paternal control. Clearly, then, his saying "my daughter, you bring sorrow to people" is not necessarily describing only that one voyeur who derived pleasure from her sight but also, and mainly, himself: He is the one harmed by her beauty, which causes him pain and anxiety about his home and his body and their borders.

R. Jose's reaction to the loss of control exposed in the voyeur's act is not to close the gap in the fence or to renounce the fantasy of controlling his daughter, but to kill her. In the story of R. Yannai and Judah, the father's wish to control his daughter's sexuality leads to the killing of the son-in-law. Here, by contrast, once the father understood that he could not exert absolute control over her sexuality and preserve it solely for himself, he decides to kill her by using a violent linguistic formulation with magical connotations—"return to your dust"—thus eliminating her latent sexual threat both to the surroundings and to himself.[16]

At a deeper level we can also envisage the possibility that the father identifies with the voyeur, who does not hesitate to "transgress" (in the full meaning of this term) and gratify his desire for the beautiful daughter through the pleasure of seeing her, even though he cannot marry her.[17] In a sense both the voyeur and the father are in the same position vis-à-vis the daughter: Neither one can marry her. If, through this act, the voyeur is conveying the desire of the father himself, this could explain the father's harsh and extreme reaction to the expression of this forbidden passion, since the father's desire for his daughter could subvert hierarchical power relationships and limit his ability to rule over his small kingdom and over his household. As Jane Gallop notes, a father's desire for his daughter could exclude him from the social world where women are objects exchanged between men in the service of communal and power relations. His desire undermines the father's ownership of his daughter, because it turns her into an object he has trouble giving up. If the father finds it hard to see his daughter as an exchangeable object—that is, giving her up to another man—then the daughter is no more his property than she is her own property.[18] Thus the very determination that the daughter must die gives control back to the father and grants him the utmost form of power, as divine power itself: the power to determine who will live and who will die. The death of the beautiful daughter will cover up the vulnerability of the father's household and will make his rule undisputable.

These two sources explicate the feeling of R. Yannai, who seems to be trapped in a similar anxious paradigm that turns him into someone who fails to distinguish fantasy from reality. Unlike his son-in-law Judah, who is split between two contradictory desires—the Torah and his wife—in the world of the father, R. Yannai, there is no such concern. He imagines that the attraction and seduction of the daughter are so compelling that no power, certainly not Torah study, could possibly prevent his son-in-law from reaching his home, and therefore he could only have been delayed by death. R. Yannai, who issues the command to lower Judah's bed, calls for a magical step that will concretize his ambivalent anxiety/desire through the death of his son-in-law. The nullification and elimination of the husband enable the father to put an end to his daughter's sexual and conjugal relations, returning her to him and to his supervision and authority, even if it means she would no longer be able to extend the family's lineage.

Meriting further emphasis is R. Yannai's identification with Judah's strong desire for his daughter, since only such an identification could explain R. Yannai's far-fetched interpretation of his son-in-law's tardiness. We can thus see hints to the father's jealousy and his desire to "get rid" of his son-in-law, who does succeed in tasting from the daughter's sexuality, unlike the father, whose incestual passion for her remains unfulfilled.[19] On the other hand, it is impossible to ignore the homoerotic dimension of the story, since R. Yannai clearly identifies not only with his son-in-law's desire for his daughter but also with his daughter's desire for her husband. In his tense wait for his son-in-law, he takes her wait upon himself, and in fact partly brings to life her missing figure within the story. This interpretation is supported by the use of the expression "lower his bed," which reminds us, even if slightly and partially, of another reversal familiar from rabbinic literature—"turning tables," a euphemism for anal sex between husband and wife.[20] Further support for such a reading can be found in a Palestinian partial version of the present story, which explicitly mentions the relationship between Judah and his father-in-law, R. Yannai, while ignoring the erotic dimension of the relationship between R. Yannai's daughter and Judah:

> Judah, the son of R. Hiyah, studied.
>
> On every Sabbath eve, he would go and inquire after his father-in-law, R. Yannai.
>
> And he [R. Yannai] would sit on a high place to see him and stand up before him.

> Once, he was late coming up.
>
> Said he [R. Yannai]: It is not possible that Judah my son changed his custom.
>
> He said: It can only be that suffering overtook the body of this righteous man. It appears that we do not have Judah.
>
> PT Bikkurim 3:3[21]

In this version of the story, despite the mention of R. Yannai as Judah's father-in-law, the relationship is only between the two of them. Judah goes to study Torah and returns every Sabbath eve (the sexual connotation here is hard to ignore) to inquire after his father-in-law. R. Yannai ascends to a high place to wait and see when his son-in-law will arrive. Here, too, Judah's death is caused by his tardiness. Contrary to the version in the Babylonian Talmud, where the explanation for Judah's delay is his immersion in his studies, in the Palestinian tradition no grounds are offered for his tardiness in the context of the plot. As in the Babylonian tradition, however, R. Yannai cannot think of any reason, except for physical suffering, which might have prevented his son-in-law from coming to visit him. And here, too, R. Yannai's anxiety, and perhaps also his guilty feelings, lead Judah to his death.

If Tal Ilan's assumption that the Babylonian tradition is an elaboration on or an expansion of the Palestinian tradition that preceded it is correct, then this Babylonian story may actually be an attempt to change or sublimate a story that basically deals with the relationship between R. Yannai and his son-in-law, Judah, with the marriage ties serving merely as a cover or a mask for the central relationship—that between the two men. Thus the Babylonian version of the story sets up a construct resembling an erotic love triangle, even as the figure of the daughter is repressed from the overt level of the narration.

In *Deceit, Desire, and the Novel,* René Girard showed that, in every such triangle, the tie between the two desiring subjects may be far stronger and more intense than that of either of them to the "legal" object of their desire—in this case, the beloved woman. Through the term "mimetic desire," Girard shows that often the very choice of the desired object is determined, from the start, not by the qualities and features of the beloved but by the fact that she is already the chosen object of another man, who serves as a rival. Girard denies the existence of "spontaneous" desire. Instead, desire for an object emerges as a product of identification with another subject ("mediator") who is interested in this object. The desiring subject adopts the desire of the other, and the rivalry with him, rather than the attraction to the desired object, becomes the main driving force in the actions and choices of the desiring subject.[22] Girard's model, however, is drawn neutrally in terms of gender, as if gender itself is meaningless within the structure he suggests. Yet he does note that fascination with the rival could definitely include a homoerotic aspect, given that the strong fixation with the rival could also create desire for him, obscuring the desire for the desired object.[23] Girard emphasizes the rival's admirable qualities and their denial by the desiring subject, who engages in self-deception about the mimetic character of his desire. The rival's mimetic desire and the attempt to cover up the enchantment with it through involvement with the desired object are frequently replaced by feelings of hostility, hatred, and the wish to "get rid" of it. This may explain R. Yannai's haste to determine that his son-in-law has died: R. Yannai's enchantment with his son-in-law and his identification with Judah's desire for his daughter mask hostility toward him as well, and a hidden wish to do away with him.

In her critical perspective on this model, Eve Kosofsky Sedgwick critiques Girard's transparent model of desire, which divests power relationships from sexual and gender categories, even though it is precisely these categories that fuel the modes of power deployment in all societies.[24] In *Between Men*, she coins the term "homosocial male desire" to imprint social bonding between men with the hallmark of erotic desire. This homosocial feature refers to social, professional, and economic ties between men. According to Sedgwick, ties often cover up unconscious homoerotic links even when, outwardly, these are normative relationships between men who are entirely unaware of the hidden erotic aspect. These alliances spread over every possible axis of male relationships: from comradeship and friendship or rivalry to mentorship, legacy, and homoerotic love. Sedgwick claims that a continuity (though denied) prevails between social and erotic ties, even when they are characterized by homophobia and misogyny. She shows that the question of women's status and that of the relationships between the sexes in general cannot be separated from the very structure of the relationships between men, even when these relationships appear to be entirely unrelated to women. Women are a vital category in the emergence of these relationships and in the strengthening and preservation of social, economic, hierarchic, and other ties between the main, male protagonists.

THE THIRD STORY

The Wedding of R. Judah ha-Nasi's Son

This story continues the trend begun in the previous one—the father regulates sexuality and conjugal ties while ignoring the daughter/daughter-in-law, who serves as a pawn in a game played by the two men attempting to control her sexuality. As in the previous story, this attempt culminates in an extreme situation leading to death. But, unlike in the previous story, where paternal control over the daughter leads to the death of the son-in-law, here an opposite act of control takes place: The drama of the father-son relationship and the father's wish to regulate the son's sexuality lead to the death of the daughter-in-law, who does not meet the rigid demands of the marital match. In fact it is not the daughter who fails here but her father. The death of the daughter/daughter-in-law is caused by a flaw in the ancestry of both fathers. According to the kinship model of Claude Lévi-Strauss, as noted, the daughter is the element that is relinquished in the exchange that takes place through the marriage. If exchanging her does not properly serve the class and patriarchal order, as in this case, she has to be subtracted from the story, even at the cost of her death. The discussion about the ancestry of the dead daughter-in-law conducted between the heads of the households substantiates anthropologist Gayle Rubin's claim that the patriarchal order rests on the use of women as exchangeable assets for the purpose of strengthening and consolidating the relationships between men.[1] From a similar perspective, feminist economist Heidi Hartmann defines patriarchy as

> relations between men, which have a material base, and which, though hierarchical, establish or create interdependence and solidarity among men that enable them to dominate women. Though patriarchy is hierarchical and men of different classes, races, or ethnic groups have different places in the patriarchy, they also are united in their shared relationship of dominance over their women; they are dependent on each other to maintain that domination.[2]

Thus the fate of the daughters-in-law mentioned in the story—the one who died and the one who was almost humiliated but was finally saved—is presented as decided entirely by the households exchanging them, while the daughters-in-law themselves, including their own views on the matter, are entirely missing.

R. Judah ha-Nasi wishes to control and take command of his son's sexuality by controlling the lives and deaths of the son's two wives, the one who had been intended for him and died, and the one he ended up marrying. By contrast with the strong-willed father, the son is revealed as weak and unable to break away from the father's authority and consummate his sexuality without his father's approval. For the son, sexuality means desire and a wish to fulfill it, whereas R. Judah ha-Nasi views sexuality as merely a means for setting up a prestigious patriarchal dynasty. The story, then, unfolds in the tension between sexuality as desire and sexuality as procreative power, as evident not only in the gap between the son's desire and the father's goals but also between the polarized roles that Rabbi intends for the women ("this one is his wife and that one his whore"). Furthermore, unlike Rav Rehumi and Judah, R. Yannai's son-in-law, the protagonists of the two previous stories who are attracted to learning more than they are attracted to their wives, and unlike the other sages presented in the chain of stories (except, perhaps, for the son studying in the seventh story), the son in this story shows absolutely no signs of a desire for learning. Studying is perceived more as an obligation (mainly toward the father) than as the will of the son, who is occupied with his desire for the woman. This story, then, illustrates the fundamental point we wish to present: In this chain of stories, the vertical intergenerational tension is no less acute than the horizontal tension between the desire for learning and the desire for the woman that stands at the center of this story. Not by chance, then, the concern with going away to study swiftly develops into a concern with questions about the vertical axis of lineage, dynasty, and status.

The drama described in the first part of the story rests on a status gap, seemingly marginal and negligible, between the family of R. Judah ha-Nasi and R. Hiyah's household. Jeffrey Rubenstein argues that, although the story's protagonists, R. Judah ha-Nasi and R. Hiyah, are from the Land of Israel, the story—which has no parallel Palestinian version—reflects the great importance that Babylonian Jews ascribed to family lineage.[3] R. Judah ha-Nasi is a descendant of Shephatyah ben Avital, King David's fifth son, who was born during the king's stay in Hebron.[4] By contrast, Rabbi viewed R. Hiyah's ancestry as flawed because he came from the family of Shimei, who was only David's brother.[5] This was not the only time the two men were involved in a tense situation around questions of status and hierarchy. Several Palestinian and Babylonian sources describe, in various ways, the tension surrounding R. Judah ha-Nasi's lineage.[6] One example is a story in the Palestinian Talmud resting on the same purist and exacting view of status and lineage. In a way, however, this story is a reverse image of the story about the match of R. Judah ha-Nasi's son, as it exposes the Achilles' heel of the purist approach when Rabbi confronts a flaw in his own lineage:

> Rabbi was very modest and used to say, "I will do whatever anyone tells me, except for what the Bnei Bathyra did for my ancestor when they removed themselves and appointed him to their office. Were Rav Huna, the *Resh Galutha*, to come up here, I would place him above me because he is descended from Judah and I from Benjamin; his descent is from the male line [of the tribe of Judah] and I am from the female line."
>
> One day, R. Hiyah the Elder came to him and said, "Rav Huna is outside."
>
> Rabbi blushed with shame.
>
> Said he [R. Hiyah to Rabbi], "His coffin is here."
>
> Said he [Rabbi to R. Hiyah], "Go, and see who is looking for you outside."
>
> He went out and found no one, and understood that he [Rabbi] was angry with him.[7]
>
> PT Kilayim 9:3

As Ofra Meir notes, the story rests on an unresolved ironic tension between the narrator's dramatic declaration—"Rabbi was very modest"—and the actual events. We learn that Rabbi's modesty fails the reality test—he fears for his honor and is unwilling to do what the Bnei Bathyra elders did when they abdicated in favor of Hillel the Elder, founder of the *nasi* dynasty to which Rabbi belongs. The source of the tension is the knowledge that, contrary to the story discussed in this chapter, Rabbi's ancestry is partial, female, and flawed.[8] Due to this sense of inadequacy, Rabbi is willing to acknowledge that if Rav Huna—the exilarch (*Resh Galutha*) with the perfect ancestry—were to arrive, he would abdicate in his favor. In a sense this declaration entails no actual commitment, given the slim chances of Rav Huna renouncing his eminent role in Babylonia to come to Palestine.[9] R. Hiyah, who himself had done so, appears in the second part of the story as a kind of trickster tasked with exposing the truth behind Rabbi's declaration.[10] For this purpose he creates a kind of cruel and amusing simulation that puts Rabbi's claim to the test and confronts him with his existential, largely status-related, anxieties. Note that, according to Rabbi, those of lower status are perceived as *nekevot* (females; a derogatory term when used in regard to males). R. Hiyah comes to Rabbi and announces, "Rav Huna is outside." He obviously neglects to mention that he is alluding to Rav Huna's coffin, which was brought to Palestine for burial, thereby pushing Rabbi to stand by his commitment and give up his leadership. Rabbi's powerful reaction to the possibility of his removal from office is primary and preverbal—"he blushed with shame"—attesting to the anxiety that took hold of him.[11] R. Hiyah's purportedly soothing remark, "His coffin is here," does remove the concrete threat to Rabbi's leadership but also emphasizes the badge of shame clinging to him as a weak man who failed to stand by his word. The short story ends by setting status matters straight: Rabbi, hurt and of higher rank than R. Hiyah, sends him outside in a kind of symbolic dismissal.[12]

Let us return to our story. R. Judah ha-Nasi's status anxiety is reaffirmed here, too, and in this case leads to the death of the girl in order to prevent any potential blemish to the purity of the patriarchal-royal dynasty to which R. Judah ha-Nasi belongs. Her violent death emphasizes that the punishment for blemishing the male side of the dynasty is actually imposed on its female side, on the one to be transferred from one family to another.[13] The atavistic fear of the woman shapes the potential bride as a kind of toxic, lethal element that could filter down through the households, "infecting" and "contaminating" a pure dynasty with the alien and unworthy genetic baggage of an inferior one and, undetected, mar its purity. The solution, then, is to identify the infectious element and destroy it immediately, as if dealing with a plague.

The dialogue between father and son concerning the proper form of sexuality is interesting and unique. At the start of the story, dealing with the choice of a suitable wife, the son is excluded from the process, which involves only the heads of the households (and in fact only Rabbi, who selects a wife for his son). The woman then passes before the son, who reveals to his father his wish to consummate his marriage before leaving for his studies. It is unclear why the bride is passed before the groom and what the purpose of this act is. Even if the purpose was to meet the requirement that appears in BT Kiddushin—"A man may not betroth a woman before seeing her, lest he [later] sees something repulsive in her and she becomes loathsome to him" (BT Kiddushin 41a)—the match here has already been determined by the father (who disqualified and killed the previous bride), and it is definitely unclear why she is passed before him twice.[14] This could be a kind of test or a type of reversed *rite de passage*, requiring the young man to display sexual restraint when confronted with direct temptation. If this is indeed a *rite de passage*, the son fails it; he cannot resist the temptation and asks to consummate the marriage first and only then leave for his studies. Note that this would be a one-time event, since he is about to absent himself from home for a long time. According to

Boyarin, one could thus claim that, in the Babylonian view, desire is not constant and ongoing but rather a single occurrence to be resolved and consummated at an early stage of the marriage.[15] The son understands that he failed the test set by his father, and therefore he is ashamed, though the shame could also be related to the actual exposure of his sexual desire to someone who is not supposed to see it—his father.

The father's reaction reveals the complexity of the situation wherein he and his son have been placed and the game of masks in which they are engaged. Ostensibly, the father should have endorsed the view that the son's shame is justified, remonstrating him for his failure to control his desire. Instead he legitimizes the son's desire, which he himself awakened. The father's positive, accepting response to the son's desire creates a subversive space where no answer is found to the question of what R. Judah ha-Nasi wanted from his son—did he want to awaken his desire? Did he want to, in some measure, visualize it and share in it? This subversive space is further intensified, given the verse that Rabbi chose to cite to validate his son's desire—a quote from the Song of Moses, praising the God who will bring his children into the Land: "Thou wilt bring them in, and plant them on thy own mountain, the place, O Lord, which thou hast made for thy abode, the sanctuary, O Lord, which thy hands have established" (Exodus 15:17). In the midrash of this verse in *Mekhilta de-Rabbi Ishmael*, the sages emphasize its underlying intergenerational aspect:

> "Thou Bringest Them In, and Plantest Them." The fathers prophesied without realizing what they prophesied. It is not written here: "Thou bringest *us* in and plantest *us*," but: "Thou bringest *them* in and plantest *them*." They thus predicted that the children would enter the land and the fathers would not.[16]

This midrash claims that, already in the Song of Moses, that is, at an early stage of the long desert journey, Moses knew that he and his contemporaries would not enter the land. Therefore he noted in his praises that others, the sons, would enter and conquer the land while he and his contemporaries would perish in the desert. Recognizing the intergenerational foundation of the verse that R. Judah ha-Nasi cites to his son underscores the intergenerational gap between them but, at the same time, enables the father to somehow share in the son's sexual desire.

Furthermore, as Dina Stein shows, in R. Judah ha-Nasi's metaphor, the son's desire to gratify his sexuality is likened to (the children's and not the fathers') religious aspiration to strike roots in the Holy Land, and the wish to marry the girl is likened to the building of a sanctuary to God. Again, the attitude toward the woman is formulated by means of religious and geographic images of place, earth, abode, sanctuary—the "home" that, once established and grounded, ensures the man not only his settlement in a fixed place but also his freedom of movement, since the woman guarantees he will have a place from which to leave and to which he can return.[17]

In the final unit of the story, the gaps of power and authority between the dominant father, R. Judah ha-Nasi, and his weak son are brought to culmination.[18] The son returns after twelve years of study, and it is then revealed that the bride is barren, seemingly due to the extended waiting period. The story opens an unbridgeable gap regarding the question of whether the son's wish was fulfilled: Did he consummate the conjugal relationship with his wife, even if only once, as hinted in his father's answer in the dialogue between them before his leaving for his long training? Or was even this one wish not fulfilled, so that the dialogue between father and son was merely a discourse of approval, affirmation, and identification—that is, a strengthening of the father-son relationship in the patriarchal setting? In any event, it is clear that the "sanctuary" that was built stands desolate, without descendants to continue the "pure dynasty" that had been so carefully preserved beforehand by keeping away the potentially infectious element. To some extent this seeming barrenness belongs to that "sterile order" that, to be maintained, required the killing of the first daughter-in-law in the story, R. Hiyah's daughter. In a way this picture is a mirror image of the flaw that required exclusion from the dynasty. The first bride was insufficiently qualified for Rabbi's dynasty, whereas the second was overqualified: Neither one can play a role in the reproduction of the male dynasty that is preoccupied with its purity.

The response to this barrenness is a kind of monologue or inner discourse that R. Judah ha-Nasi conducts with himself when examining his options for action. It should be emphasized that the son, the barren woman's husband, is not at all a partner to these misgivings, continuing the trend woven into the story from the start whereby the authority and discretion regarding the son's conjugal life are absolutely within the father's purview. R. Judah ha-Nasi raises the possibility of bringing in another woman, a third one, into the relationship, but rejects it mainly for reasons of public appearances and fears about "what will people say." The claim "If we divorce her, it will be said—the poor soul waited in vain. If he marries yet another woman, it will be said, this one is his wife and that one his whore," suggests that adopting either one of these solutions will expose the son's conjugal life not only to the scrutiny of the father but also to that of the entire community.[19] In principle, the option R. Judah ha-Nasi considers implies the splitting of the female identity between saint and whore: between the first, older wife who becomes a "whore" because she cannot have children (meaning that her sole purpose is to satisfy the husband's sexual cravings) and the new, fertile wife whose purpose is to bear children.[20]

In the end the solution to R. Judah ha-Nasi's dilemma—seeking mercy for her fertility to be restored—is a kind of *deus ex machina*. This is also the case in the next story, about Ben Hakhinai, who compels a miraculous solution to the plot by means of God's mercy, as well as in the preceding story, about R. Yannai, who compels death on his son-in-law by means of verbal magic. The very fact that this simple, easy resolution (healing the woman by means of God's mercy) is presented as a solution a posteriori—and is not meant for the woman's welfare and wellbeing but instead to prevent a public scandal that would harm the people involved—reinforces the violent facet of R. Judah ha-Nasi's character which surrounds the entire story and again highlights the fate of the first daughter-in-law. R. Judah ha-Nasi is willing to use his magical power to heal his daughter-in-law only after he imagines the alternative option: the creation of a dual conjugal relationship for his son where the woman is split into two separate female figures—the saint and the whore. In fact, a role reversal occurs here. The older spouse, who has been married to him for twelve years, is the one Rabbi describes as a "whore" because she cannot bear children, whereas the new wife, who exists only in Rabbi's imagination, is the domestic wife, who realizes her calling as a fitting spouse and is therefore defined by him as "his wife."

This reversed split in R. Judah ha-Nasi's imagination evokes the ancient split of the woman's image into the figures of Eve and Lilith, the archetypes of a motherly, submissive woman contrasting with a sexual, seductive, and threatening one. Eve, "the mother of all life," serves as a paradigm of fertility, procreation, motherhood, and survival of the male dynasty. By contrast, the sexual and seductive Lilith is painted as the negation of motherhood because she harms babies in their cradles and gives birth to demons; her motherhood, rather than being subordinate to the proper patriarchal dynasty, strives to undermine it.[21] The split construed by R. Judah ha-Nasi also emphasizes the inability to imagine a kind of womanhood that combines sexuality and motherhood. Ostensibly, in the male perception, a woman who cannot be a mother must be sexual, and a sexual woman must be a whore.

According to Freud, the sharp, conscious contrast between motherhood and sexuality originates in childhood following the initial acquaintance with the mystery of adult sexuality. The purpose of the split is "to save" the pure image of the mother, as the child perceives it, from the terror and humiliation that, in this perception, is associated with sexual activity. This is an unconscious defensive split that creates two contradictory trends—"motherly" love and tenderness versus "slutty" sensuality and sexuality. In adulthood the two trends may coalesce and be directed toward one single woman, but the split often becomes a fixation, and the man goes on distinguishing between the mother and whore types as two separate female figures.[22]

Rabbi's definition of the barren woman—who contributes nothing to the reproduction of the dynasty—as a whore is decisive. It enables him to divert attention from the man's responsibility (first and foremost himself, who sent his son away to study for so long) for the breakdown of the dynasty while indirectly assigning responsibility for it to the woman (as the first daughter-in-law had supposedly been responsible for her flawed ancestry and died, even though she had never sinned). Her definition as a whore, then, hints at her moral flaw, and it is what isolates her in her barrenness. At the same time, the whore metaphor enables Rabbi to subject her to the exchange arrangement that helps to sustain the patriarchal power. The expected public scandal, however, could potentially stain Rabbi's hallowed dynasty; therefore the sole way to prevent the blemish is "to save" the woman and return her fertility to her. Just as the first daughter-in-law had to die so as not to tarnish the male dynasty, so the second daughter-in-law had to be saved to protect it.

The split between saint and whore that R. Judah ha-Nasi sees in the woman's role strengthens the many similarities between this story and that of Tamar and Judah (Genesis 38). In a sense the hurdles Rabbi's son surmounts on the way to a proper married life are a gender reversal of those Tamar surmounts—her dead husbands, Er and Onan—until she becomes part of Judah's honorable patriarchal dynasty and contributes her significant share, which will lead to the birth of King David.[23] Like the first daughter-in-law, who died because of an unsuitable match that would have blemished the dynasty's honor, the deaths of Er and Onan are tied to their father's unsuitable choice of a match—Judah's marriage to a Canaanite woman, which ran against the accepted pattern in his father's household (as indicated in the verse "Judah went down from his brothers" [Genesis 38:1]). Just as there is a prolonged delay of sexual consummation in the life of Rabbi's son, so too is there a delay in Tamar's life, since her husband Onan wastes his seed and does not engage in sexual intercourse with her. Like R. Judah ha-Nasi, who is troubled by the question of the patriarchal dynasty, Judah, too, emerges as someone attempting to mold his dynasty according to his own considerations, even if this implies ignoring the levirate rules and abdicating his responsibility for his son's widow. Similarly, like Rabbi in his perception of R. Hiyah's daughter, Judah, too, sees Tamar as an infectious element whose removal will improve the male dynasty he wishes to head. Tamar's swift transition from a woman who "has played the whore and . . . is pregnant as a result of whoredom," and who faces death by burning ("And Judah said, 'Bring her out, and let her be burned'" [Genesis 38:24]), to the status of a righteous mother ("Then Judah acknowledged them and said, 'She is more in the right than I'" [Genesis 38:26]) parallels Rabbi's decision to dismiss the signaling of his son's wife as a whore and, in one stroke, signal her instead as a wife and mother and save her from barrenness. These transitions sharpen the split between the sexual, desired woman on the one hand and the mother on the other, even when they blend in the very same woman. The similarity to the story of Tamar and Judah attests above all to Rabbi's indirect, concealed participation in the consummation of his son's sexual match. The biblical Judah is the one who, in the end, unknowingly impregnates his daughter-in-law, his son's wife, in relations that consummate the father's hidden incestuous desire and his sexual rivalry with his sons. In that sense R. Judah ha-Nasi's absolute control over his son's sexual-matching arrangements—separating or bringing the spouses together as he wishes, killing the woman or returning her fertility to her as he wishes—enables him to satisfy his desire in sublimated, indirect ways, and to participate as a kind of secret agent in his son's desire and in its gratification.

THE FOURTH STORY

R. Hanania b. Hakhinai, His Daughter, and His Wife

Here, too, as in the previous story, is a description of a young man leaving to study Torah immediately after a wedding feast, and here, too, for a twelve-year absence. Twelve as a typological number serves as a key axis of the plot in the four stories at the center of the series—the third, fourth, fifth, and sixth.[1] The opening and closing stories in the entire narrative sequence deal with shorter absences: Rav Rehumi in the first story returned home every year; Rav Judah in the second story returned every week on the eve of the Sabbath; and in the last story, Rav Yosef, Rava's son, was supposed to be absent for six years but was overcome by longing and returned home after only three. An editorial choice seems evident here, placing the stories of more prolonged absences—where the drama of distance, separation, and longing reaches a peak—at the core of the narrative sequence. In these four stories, which deal with extended absences, a trend is also apparent suggesting absences become longer and their effects more intense. R. Judah ha-Nasi's son is described as hesitating about such a prospective long absence, and sexual relations may have been consummated before he went away to study. In the story discussed in this chapter, Ben Hakhinai goes away to study for twelve years, but his leave is described as hurried and even as beginning with a forbidden act: his abandonment of a groom at his wedding feast. In the next story, about R. Hama b. Bisa, the twelve-year study absence appears in the exposition of the story and is described matter-of-factly, implying it was something entirely natural. The sixth story, about R. Akiva, describes even two twelve-year periods of study, which his wife supports—indeed she pushes him into the first period and encourages the second.

This story, involving sages, presents a new relationship unknown to us so far. Ben Hakhinai, a friend of R. Shimon b. Yohai, attends the latter's wedding celebration, but his failure to wait for the groom goes beyond questions of politeness and propriety in a relationship between friends. Protecting the groom is an important task, and Ben Hakhinai's abandoning his friend at the liminal time of the wedding feast, a period of transition, entails real danger. R. Judah's determination in BT Berakhot emphasizes the liminal, dangerous space where the groom is found: "Rav Judah said, 'Three require protection: a sick person, a groom, and a bride. It was taught in a *beraita*, a sick person, a woman in confinement, a groom, and a bride. Some say, also a mourner, and others add, also scholars at night'" (BT Berakhot 54b). Within this protective setting, the groom's friends who accompany him on the days of the wedding feast have special halakhic standing as *bnei huppah*. Their role is to accompany the groom, guard him, and make him happy over the seven days of the feast.[2] Ben Hakhinai's act seemingly shows contempt for the institution of marriage—a contempt that makes his ardent desire for study, to the point of refusing to delay it even slightly, appear rather dubious. This attitude also has implications for his relationships with his wife and daughter, as they are presented in the rest of the story. Ben Hakhinai's unwillingness to wait for his friend is, in a way, a breach of basic cultural and halakhic norms. Indeed it serves as the driving force of the plot, exposing its protagonists to the risks that follow from this abandonment.[3]

The description of Ben Hakhinai's return to his city intensifies the odyssey element of the story. Ben Hakhinai returns to a city where nothing is known to him—neither the city streets nor his daughter. Unlike the story of Odysseus returning home, where the existential identity riddle is on a single level (Odysseus does recognize his city, his home, and his wife, but they, except for the old servant, do not recognize him), here, at least at the first stage of his return, the identity riddle is twofold: The father does not recognize his city and his daughter, and the daughter neither recognizes nor sees her father. The peak in the drama of Ben Hakhinai's return is his identification of his daughter by the river as she is drawing water. Like Odysseus, who sneaks into his home under a false identity as a poor man, Ben Hakhinai also chooses to return home without identifying himself to his relatives.[4] And indeed, his arrival home is a complete surprise, except that his wife recognizes him immediately. The surprise element turns tragic when the wife dies of shock, a death her husband successfully reverses.[5]

One prominent issue in the story is that the father and daughter never recognize one another. Ben Hakhinai does not identify his daughter on his own; instead he learns who she is when her name (which invokes only his name) is mentioned loudly by others. This is the "father's name" in a Lacanian sense, an issue we discuss at length in the next story. In the present context, it means that fatherhood remains in place so long as it is expressed in a name. In that sense, Ben Hakhinai's physical absence from his home does not tarnish his symbolic power as a father, which is greater than the physical father's real power. And yet the enormous gap between the actual estrangement of father and daughter and the symbolic closeness between them—denoted by a name—stresses the inappropriateness, and indeed the tragic quality, of the split between reality and symbol.

The story uses a biblical type-scene (in Robert Alter's terms) of a girl drawing water while a stranger observes her, a well-known tableau charged with distinctive erotic implications.[6] Rebekah draws water for Abraham's servant and for his camels, and thereby proves that she is a suitable wife for his master's son, Isaac:

> He made the camels kneel down outside the city by the well of water; it was toward evening, the time when women go out to draw water. And he said, "O Lord, God of my master Abraham, please grant me success today and show steadfast love to my master Abraham. I am standing here by the spring of water, and the daughters of the townspeople are coming out to draw water. Let the girl to whom I shall say, 'Please offer your jar that I may drink,' and who shall say, 'Drink, and I will water your camels'—let her be the one whom you have appointed for your servant Isaac. By this I shall know that you have shown steadfast love to my master." Before he had finished speaking, there was Rebekah, who was born to Bethuel son of Milcah, the wife of Nahor, Abraham's brother, coming out with her water jar on her shoulder. The girl was very fair to look upon, a virgin, whom no man had known. She went down to the spring, filled her jar, and came up. Then the servant ran to meet her and said, "Please let me sip a little

> water from your jar." "Drink, my lord," she said, and quickly lowered her jar upon her hand and gave him a drink. When she had finished giving him a drink, she said, "I will draw for your camels also, until they have finished drinking." So she quickly emptied her jar into the trough and ran again to the well to draw, and she drew for all his camels.
>
> Genesis 24: 11–20

Jacob first meets Rachel by the well's mouth:

> Now when Jacob saw Rachel, the daughter of his mother's brother Laban, and the sheep of his mother's brother Laban, Jacob went up and rolled the stone from the well's mouth, and watered the flock of his mother's brother Laban. Then Jacob kissed Rachel, and wept aloud. And Jacob told Rachel that he was her father's kinsman, and that he was Rebekah's son; and she ran and told her father. When Laban heard the news about his sister's son Jacob, he ran to meet him; he embraced him and kissed him, and brought him to his house. Jacob told Laban all these things.
>
> Genesis 29: 10–13

Moses, too, meets Zipporah, his future wife, by a well in Midian:

> When Pharaoh heard of it, he sought to kill Moses. But Moses fled from Pharaoh. He settled in the land of Midian, and sat down by a well. The priest of Midian had seven daughters. They came to draw water, and filled the troughs to water their father's flock. But some shepherds came and drove them away. Moses got up and came to their defense and watered their flock. When they returned to their father Reuel, he

> said, "How is it that you have come back so soon today?" They said, "An Egyptian helped us against the shepherds; he even drew water for us and watered the flock." He said to his daughters, "Where is he? Why did you leave the man? Invite him to break bread." Moses agreed to stay with the man, and he gave Moses his daughter Zipporah in marriage. She bore a son, and he named him Gershom; for he said, "I have been an alien [*ger*] residing in a foreign land."
>
> Exodus 2: 15–22

The three biblical traditions entailing a meeting by the well deal directly with the connections among masculinity, water-drawing as a feminine practice, marriage matches, and erotic fulfillment. The difference between the tradition about Rebekah and Abraham's servant and the two others—about Jacob and Rachel and about Moses and Zipporah—is that the latter two include an act involving proof of physical prowess: Jacob rolls the stone from the well's mouth, and Moses protects the right of Reuel's (Yithro's) daughters to draw water. No masculine physical sign appears in the first story because Rebekah is not meant for the old servant of Abraham but for his absent son, Isaac, who cannot show proof of his strength, neither here nor anywhere else.[7]

The story of Abraham's servant and Rebekah also emphasizes the issue of chance, thereby suggesting the role of fate. Indeed the water-drawing scene as a whole is one of fate: In all three stories the girl drawing water is the right one and the best suited to the hero, with their match reflecting divine will. According to a similar mechanism, the first girl to meet Ben Hakhinai on his return will obviously be his own daughter. And, as in the story of Jacob and Rachel, their encounter is a reunification of relatives who meet again after being separated, even though in fact they have never met before.

Contrary to the biblical stories, where water drawing leads to explicitly erotic conclusions that culminate in marriage and progeny, here the erotic possibility between Ben Hakhinai and his daughter is not realized, though it is not entirely dismissed, either. The very scene of their encounter, according to the outline of the biblical narratives, enables the story to hint at hidden or repressed erotic content. So also do their names in the story—"Ben Hakhinai" (son of Hakhinai) and "daughter of Hakhinai"— blur the generational gap between them. They are presented as a kind of couple, on the one hand, and on the other, they concretize and intensify the experience of the absent father, since "Hakhinai" is not his own name but that of his father. The daughter's ascription to the grandfather rather than to the father creates a dual movement: the disappearance of the real father and his transgressive creation as a kind of brother to his daughter.

From the moment Ben Hakhinai discovers that the girl drawing water is his daughter, no dialogue—either verbal or physical—takes place between them. Had Ben Hakhinai presented himself to her as her father, and had he accompanied her to their home, not only would this have restricted the erotic possibility that emerged by the river but the mother's death would have been avoided as well. The daughter could have prepared the mother for his arrival, creating a proper and structured scene of return. Instead of telling his daughter, however, Ben Hakhinai decides not to set the family hierarchy straight by identifying himself to her; he slyly follows her until she arrives home, and only there does he reveal himself—not to her, but to his wife. This leads to the mother's death (even if only for a moment). His unwillingness to set things back in place within the family and his persistent tracking of his daughter lead to the family tragedy, which he fixes with his magical powers.

Ben Hakhinai's actions could hint at an erotic charge concealed in the story. The meeting place by the river at the time of drawing water is reminiscent, as noted, of the biblical scenes of fate and matching, but let us not forget that water itself has a symbolic erotic meaning of flow and vitality. Characterizing the daughter is a full jar, which signifies her as bursting with youth and sexuality, particularly in contrast with her mother, whose character is shaped by the act of sifting flour. In the first case it is an act of refilling with a liquid substance, and in the second, an act of pouring and sifting (meaning subtracting) a dry substance. This counterposition of mother and daughter indirectly hints that, in the many years that have elapsed since Ben Hakhinai left his home, the mother has wilted and withered, and the daughter has now taken her place as the erotic figure in the home.[8] In that sense, the mother's sudden death actively conveys the father's forbidden desire that the daughter should inherit her mother's role, helping to explain his bizarre decision to refrain from admitting his identity to his daughter before the disaster. The mother's revival following the father's pleas represents the rejection of the forbidden erotic option as well as the return of the proper order, all without detracting from the father's power.

This story, too, like most of the stories in the series, has a parallel Palestinian version that appears in Genesis Rabba:

> Hanania b. Hakhinai and R. Shimon b. Yohai went to study Torah with R. Akiva in Bnei Brak and stayed there thirteen years.
>
> R. Shimon b. Yohai sent letters to his home and knew what [happened] there. R. Hanania b. Hakhinai did not send letters to his home and did not know what [happened] there.

> His [Hanania's] wife sent and said, "Your daughter has grown up, come and give her away in marriage."
>
> R. Akiva, who envisaged the Holy Spirit, said, "Whoever has a grown-up daughter should go and give her away in marriage."
>
> What did he [Hanania] do? He went to the well and heard the maids drawing water saying, "Daughter of Hakhinai, fill up your jar and go."
>
> She went, and he followed her until she reached her home. His wife had hardly managed to see him before her soul left her, and some say it [her soul] returned.
>
> Genesis Rabba 95[9]

Despite the strong similarity between the parallel versions, the Palestinian one appears to suggest several changes that are significant for the current discussion.[10] In the Babylonian version, the conflict at the opening of the story is between two friends—Ben Hakhinai, who refuses to be delayed until the end of R. Shimon b. Yohai's wedding feast, and the groom. Ben Hakhinai thereby conveys his view on the importance of marriage versus the greater importance of Torah study. By contrast, in the Palestinian tradition, the gap between the two is revealed at a later stage, when both are already married and have children: R. Shimon b. Yohai diligently sends letters to inquire after the members of his household, whereas Ben Hakhinai is not interested in their welfare and does not know what is happening in his home.[11] Even when his wife addresses him directly, demanding his return home to marry off his daughter, he ignores the request, and only R. Akiva's authority leads him to go back. The description of his return home is similar in both traditions, although the report in the Palestinian version about the father going home to give away in marriage the daughter he does not know heightens the tension between them, which culminates in the picture of the father tracking his daughter. Another significant difference between the two versions concerns the description of the mother's revival in the Palestinian version: "His wife had hardly managed to see him before her soul left her, and some say it [her soul] returned." Moreover, her revival, if it happened, is not explained by any steps taken by Ben Hakhinai or by God's intervention in her favor.

The mother's horrifying panic at the sight of her husband, ending in a swift and sudden death, appears as a traumatic reaction that powerfully concretizes the tragic aspect of the father's prolonged absence and the mutual loss it entails. This traumatic response is related to the shock of the surprising encounter between two different time dimensions thrust at one another: the calendrical time of the formal clock, which is measured in hours, years, and set dates (external uncontrollable time, indifferent to the needs and experiences of those subject to it) on the one hand and, on the other, inner time, measured in a private frequency according to the experiences of individuals and to the personal meaning they ascribe to it. While Ben Hakhinai's daughter grew up slowly within the mother's space and the time dimensions charted in the circles of the home and its surroundings, the father's calendric time (twelve whole years) entirely missed the full course of the mother's time movement. Since the father is absent, formal time remains outside the domestic context and internally irrelevant to it. Its sudden and alien intrusion into the family space and into the time of the mother and daughter (embodied, again, in the round and recurrent movements of drawing water and sifting flour) suddenly exposes the prolonged loss, and is thus experienced as traumatic and leading to a breakdown.[12]

Judith Baskin's comment directs attention to the connection between the ending of the story considered in this chapter and the plot of Euripides' play *Alcestis*: "It is interesting that in this story it is the wife who dies, rather like the noble wife in Euripides' play *Alcestis* who sacrifices herself to save her culpable husband. And, as in *Alcestis*, divine intervention on behalf of the husband permits the wife to return to life."[13] Euripides' play is in fact an adaptation of a well-known myth about Alcestis available in several versions: Alcestis, the wife of Admetos, sacrifices herself to save the life of her husband whom the Moirai (Fates) have sentenced to death. The Moirai stated that Admetos could be saved if someone else were willing to die in his place. After his father refuses to do so, viewing this request as beyond the bounds of his parental role, his wife, Alcestis, volunteers to die for him because she thinks his life is more important than hers: "Because I give you the place of honor and have caused you to look on the light instead of me, I am dying."[14] Immediately after her death, she is miraculously saved and resuscitated by Persephone, who returns her from her descent to Hades. In another version, which Euripides adopted, Heracles, who is there as a guest of Admetos, wrestles with the gods and brings her back to life.[15]

According to Aharon Shabtai, the play deals with what he calls "the myth of selfishness," wherein Admetos has no hesitations about sacrificing his wife to save his own life, thereby turning the myth of love into a "sequence of selfish and narcissistic considerations."[16] As Baskin notes, it is obviously impossible to speak of a dialogue between the myth of Alcestis or Euripides' play and the talmudic story.[17] Nevertheless, the similar narrative foundation strengthens and emphasizes the man's readiness to sacrifice his wife (as well as the rest of his family), even if only for a moment, on the altar of his intellectual desires, as well as the place of the woman as the one who pays the price for the husband's narcissistic longings.

Alcestis—like Ben Hakhinai's wife—is sacrificed after she has fulfilled her childbearing role and is beyond her fertile stage; thus the parallel between the stories also emphasizes the mother-daughter rivalry at the hidden level of the talmudic story, and the repression of erotic layers related to the nascent sexuality of the daughter who is meant to replace the older mother.

THE FIFTH STORY

R. Hama b. Bisa

R. Hama—like Ben Hakhinai and the son of R. Judah ha-Nasi in the two previous stories and R. Akiva in the next one—spends twelve years at the study house and then returns home. The father's appearance here, as in other stories in the series, is the sudden emergence of an absent, vanished figure in the family setting. Unlike the mother, who is described in these stories in terms of a sequence of actions (waiting, educating the children, and so forth), the father's appearance is dramatic and forceful, and includes his encroaching into the family's accepted order as it had been constituted over the years.

When R. Hama returns home, his wish is to prevent what had happened to Ben Hakhinai (in the previous story), whose surprising appearance killed his wife, even if temporarily. Hence he sends word to announce to his household that he has arrived. Unlike in the case of Ben Hakhinai, however, who tracks his daughter without her knowledge, the drama of the encounter in the present story focuses first on the study house and then at the home. According to Yona Fraenkel, the gap between these two spaces is unbridgeable.[1] While the messenger is proceeding to his home, R. Hama enters the study house and, immediately after him, so does his son, R. Oshayah. According to the story, they do not recognize one another, and a unique and bizarre situation emerges, where father and son study Torah together as two complete strangers.

Scholars who have dealt with father-son relationships in rabbinic literature have pointed out the complexity of these ties. Fraenkel focused mainly on the effects of the absence on the father.[2] Daniel Boyarin noted the father's strong desire to turn his son into, in a way, his intellectual doppelganger, thereby overcoming his own fear of death and founding an ongoing male hereditary line that preserves the continuity of Jewish existence.[3] This approach is prominent in the story about the strange and complex relationship between R. Shimon b. Yohai and his son R. Eliezer, which culminates in R. Shimon b. Yohai's decision to hide in a cave for thirteen years with his son, shielding him from any external influence and attempting to create, in quasi-laboratory conditions of isolation, his perfect clone.[4] Evident in these stories, however, is also a strong awareness that this longing for an intellectual legacy and for children will meet with failure. The strength of the father's desire to bring up and educate his son in his image prevents him from seeing his son as a separate individual. Thus the son opposes his father's plan and strives to create a new and private space for himself that is often far removed from the anxious father's realm of influence. Sons do ultimately make their way toward the father, but for that to happen, the intervention of a "benefactor" is required. This is a character external to the family drama, who is not caught in the father's anxieties and is therefore capable of mediating, according to Dina Stein, between the biological father and the son's needs and desires. This mediation eventually allows the son, as an adult and independent person, to reach the place the father had intended for him to begin with and to become a scholar. As Stein notes, this benefactor can be a member of the community, such as an important rabbi, or a figure enjoying high prestige in it, such as the prophet Elijah.[5]

In the story discussed in this chapter, a unique equivalence is seemingly created between the father and the benefactor who teaches the son Torah. Paradoxically, it is precisely the father's absence—the fact that he does not know his son or what he looks like and has never studied with him—that enables the fulfillment of the sages' quest for continuity. The father's sadness when confronting this brilliant student is conveyed in his statement, "Had I been here, I would have had such a child." In Fraenkel's view, this statement discloses the complexity of the father's place in the process of the son's upbringing, given that "the father holds it is impossible without him, whereas in truth he is redundant."[6] A slightly more precise formulation of Fraenkel's comment is required. The real father is redundant, but the imagined father, the father whom the son construes as studying Torah in some distant *beth midrash*, is not only not redundant but also necessary. The son's success and his turning into such an exact successor of the father follow precisely from the fact that the real father was never there to bring him up.

A comparative reading of this and the second story (about R. Yannai, the father who waits for his daughter's husband) clarifies the depth of the difference between the father-son relationship and the father-daughter relationship in the talmudic narrative. Clearly, the expectation from the son is that he will grow up and develop through individuation and separation from the father, and R. Hama's prolonged absence is, in a way, a geographic and temporal concretization of this basic separation idea. By contrast the daughter lacks any possibility of a separate existence, to the point of not even being represented on her own in the story but merely contained within the father's gaze. The Ben Hakhinai story does not assign a name or a voice of her own to the daughter, and certainly no mutual recognition between her and her father. Her identity is reduced to her being "his daughter."

The end of the story exposes the gap between the imagined father, who can serve as a beneficial and nurturing figure for the son, and the real father. R. Hama, who has by now arrived home and met his wife, sees the scholar he had met at the *beth midrash* arriving at his house. To honor him, he stands up, expecting to continue the learning experience they had shared, "thinking he had come to ask him a question." His wife, who immediately understands what is happening, sets the hierarchical order straight—"Is there a father who stands up before his son?"—and tries to move the father from the imagined to the real dimension to restore the proper social and familial order. Inadvertently, however—since she does not know about their previous study together—the mother undermines the brief learning idyll they had shared and the father cannot really honor the son for his learning and erudition.

In fact R. Oshayah was brought up and educated by a father whose power is greater than that of any other: the absent father, who withdrew to the *beth midrash* and is therefore identified in the son's perception with the institution and the discourse it represents. Classic psychoanalysis ascribes great importance to the father's absent function and views it as a vital element in the child's development. In many ways the father is absent to begin with, since fatherhood itself is merely a symbolic concept, an assumption based on an abstraction. In Freud's words, "maternity is proved by the senses whereas paternity is a surmise based on a deduction and a premise."[7] Unlike motherhood, fatherhood lacks a distinct bodily form; it is invisible and cannot be visually concretized. Since there is no way of showing that a specific child is the descendant of one or another man, or of any man at all, the family ties between the father and his children rest on the mother's testimony.[8] R. Hama can identify his son only when his wife explicitly attests to it: "Is there a father who stands up before his son?" Fatherhood, then, is a structure resting on the word, not the flesh. It always transcends specific physical concreteness and, therefore, attains symbolic status. Nancy Chodorow writes about the existence of the father as a fantastic character in the child's inner life: Since the father is identified with the cultural life outside and is often absent from the domestic space, he is less connected to the setting of the child's object relations and becomes a character the child needs to imagine more than experience.[9]

Behind the recognition of the fatherly function, then, is symbolization, as a vital mental process and a necessary component of entry into the culture. Following Freud, Jacques Lacan sets up the father as the one who signifies entry into the symbolic order, evident in the acquisition of language and in social integration: The father is the one who represents command of language, of law and proscription, of discourse, and of consciousness. His image transcends its specific physical concretization and is embodied in all aspects of the patriarchal structure. According to Lacan, fatherhood as a whole is based on the "paternal metaphor," which identifies the father with the law.[10] Within the "paternal metaphor" the father represents the law and, from it, builds meaning and assigns the subject an identity and a position in the symbolic order. His representative, metaphoric-symbolic function, then, is vital to the consolidation of the subjective identity.

The very perception of the father in cultural terms thus rests on the denial of his body—on the negation of his physical, material, and limited existence—in order to ascribe to him a quality of general abstraction and tie him to the spiritual constructs of law and language. This allows the range of his power and influence to expand without any limitations of physicality, specificity, or time and place.

This possibility of rising beyond the physical being, of existing as an abstract entity, incorporeal and nonspecific, ties the power of the father to the power of God: Belief in a hidden God who cannot be apprehended with the senses resembles the belief that a specific man is a father to his child, despite the absence of any sensorial evidence. In both cases, power and control are obviously ascribed to the one who succeeds in concealing his body: The more the father, like God, rises above his physical, corporeal, concrete existence—that is, the more he is absent from his body but present and existent as a concept (like R. Hama, who is absent from his home for twelve years)—the stronger his symbolic status, which functions more efficiently precisely because it is unbound by time and space limits.

Possibly, then, R. Oshayah is such an impressive scholar precisely because his father was so absent—that is, because of his effective and unlimited training by the symbolic father, as represented by Torah study. No wonder then that, as soon as the father returns and is embodied in a physical presence, the power arrangements in the family are entirely distorted. The father who appears in a vulnerable body and in historical reality is no longer a father whose hegemony is impervious to all harm, and his symbolic power is suddenly weakened: "[He] saw that his [R. Oshayah's] answers were wise. He was dismayed." The distortion is also evident in the inference that the father wishes to resemble his son instead of the son attempting to imitate the father—after all, the father also operates within the same space of the real and the imagined. He too has a "real" and an "imagined" self, and his desire to resemble his son is actually a desire to negate his own (invariably flawed) reality dimension and uphold instead the imagined dimension reflected in the perception of his son. A kind of "retrospective dynasty" emerges here, which calls for restabilization.

The weakness and the subversion of the power balance are physically represented when the father rises before his son. Only the woman, in her "lack," can set the proper sequence in place. The mother's testimony—the wonder of R. Hama b. Bisa's wife at her husband's behavior—resets fatherhood on the symbolic axis and enables its fixation through the use of a proverb in a biblical verse, including its supporting authority, "A threefold cord is not quickly broken" (Ecclesiastes 4:12). This verse emphasizes the strength of the male genealogy—from grandfather to father to son—and the absence of women from it:[11] "this is R. Oshayah, son of R. Hama, son of Bisa." The father, who until that moment had viewed himself as a failed father, is now reaffirmed in his hegemonic status and plants himself at the center of the generational threesome, a key axis in transmitting the legacy of wisdom—even though he had not actively participated in this transmission. This is an ideal, imagined dynasty, which is created ex post facto with the revelation that the alien sage is none other than his actual son. This reaffirmation serves R. Hama as a retrospective justification for his very absence and prolonged stay at the *beth midrash*, given that it had obviously not prevented, and had even encouraged, the growth of R. Oshayah as a scholar who brings pride and honor to his father. The story, then, underscores the structured, symbolic, and imagined dimension of the male dynasty that ostensibly should have been perceived as obvious and self-evident.

THE SIXTH STORY

R. Akiva's Family

This story describes two family circles: It opens with Ben Kalba Savu'a, who vows to disinherit his daughter immediately after she chooses a spouse he considers unworthy of her, and ends with R. Akiva's daughter, who emulates her mother and marries Ben Azzai, a man who does not want to be married and only wants to study Torah.

The story, which appears in a slightly different version in BT Nedarim,[1] describes the daughter of Ben Kalba Savu'a, who chooses the shepherd Akiva for a husband. Although her father disowns her, she becomes betrothed to Akiva, sends him away to study Torah, and meets him again only twenty-four years later, when he is a great and famous rabbi and has twenty-four thousand disciples of his own.[2] Yona Fraenkel views this story as a paradigm of perfect spiritual harmony between Akiva and his wife:

> Every Jew who lived in the study house of the talmudic sages undoubtedly knew that R. Akiva is among the greatest of

> Torah authorities and that he is the pillar the entire Oral Law rests upon. . . . All these—the narrator says—come from "her," from one Jewish woman, poor and abandoned, but united in her soul with her husband in the study house.[3]

Shulamit Valler adds to Fraenkel's comment and suggests a romantic-naive reading of the story that sees the woman as a "full partner" to the wishes and actions of R. Akiva, leaving no room for holding that this led to her distress. Quite the contrary, in her view "the story is entirely optimistic": The woman stands at the center and inspires her husband, and thus the will of R. Akiva is actually her own will. In Valler's view, "the sage's long absence harmed neither love nor family harmony."[4] This approach follows from her broader claim that, for the entire chain of stories, "the solution is based on partnership and understanding between husband and wife, not on the model of the wife as the obedient lamb."[5] Tal Ilan, too, sees this story as emblematic of a woman's loyalty to her absent husband, and even compares R. Akiva's wife and her perseverance in waiting for his return to Penelope's wait for the return of Odysseus (who was away from his home for a similar period—twenty years).[6]

Contrary to Fraenkel, Valler, and others who hold an optimistic view of the story, Daniel Boyarin finds it hard to see harmony and partnership in a conjugal relationship that in fact remains unfulfilled for twenty-four years. Instead he sees the male creation of a utopian woman who encourages her spouse to remain absent as much as he wishes and never complains about it. According to Boyarin, this was the solution to the tension between the conjugal relationship and the desire for study—shaping the image of R. Akiva's wife as an "ideal for Jewish womanhood."[7] In his view the text of the Babylonian Talmud "proposes then a sort of utopian solution, which allows for both marriage and total commitment to Torah-study, namely, marrying early and then leaving home for extended periods of time to study Torah. In short, the solution of the Babylonian culture was to create a class of married monks."[8] In the story of R. Akiva and his wife, he sees a narrative reincarnation of the metaphor about the ideal marriage bond between a man and a woman as the relationship between shepherd and ewe (*rehelah*). This model is further strengthened through the close repetition of the narrative structure adopted in the biblical story of Jacob and Rachel (the similarity in the names is not random): "There also, the hero is a shepherd in love with his master's daughter. There also, the father opposes the match. There also, the shepherd works for two periods of a number of years to win her."[9]

Boyarin's analysis, however, seems to miss the fundamental difference between the story of Jacob and Rachel and that of R. Akiva and his wife. In the talmudic story the wife/daughter is the one who, for two long periods (twice twelve years), engages in traditional woman's "work"—waiting and hoping to finally win favor in the eyes of her husband/lover. These gender substitutions reinforce even further the radical idealization of female waiting and the creation of Akiva's mythological figure as a desired paragon of a Torah scholar in ways that best serve the male interest.

The tension and ambivalence surrounding the long wait of R. Akiva's wife are also discernible in her answer to her neighbors' suggestion that she should borrow some suitable clothes to wear for his arrival, which she rejects, citing half a verse from Proverbs: "A righteous man knows the soul of his beast" (Proverbs 12:10). The very act of citing and the content of the verse turn her brief response into a complex space that moves along the spectrum of compliance with hierarchical patriarchal norms and considerable opposition to them.[10]

The very choice of R. Akiva's wife (or perhaps the choice of the narrator) to use a verse, a holy text, the same text that she sent him to study, makes her an equal to her absent husband. She, too, even though she did not go away to study, knows how to cite verses and use them in complex ways. Even so, the verse cited points to hierarchy and relies on the relationship between an owner and his beast. The owner is indeed presented in the verse as one who "knows": He is caring, understanding, and sensitive to the beast's needs but still acknowledges the clear hierarchical gap between the two. In an analogy to the relationship suggested in the verse, R. Akiva is the owner, his wife is the beast, and he "knows her soul." Hence his wife's refraining from borrowing clothes follows from her desire to have her husband see her as she is. She is not interested in wearing a disguise for him, hiding her decay, her degradation, and the harsh years she has lived through. She wants R. Akiva, who has not met her in twenty-four years, to see her as she is and to respect the enormous price she was required to pay to create for him an intellectual sphere that is free for study.[11]

By contrast, "knows" is also tied to the question of identification. Despite the drama of the late return and in diametrical contrast to the events in *The Odyssey*, she "knows" that R. Akiva "will know"; that is, he will identify her and recognize her immediately, regardless of the long time that has elapsed. Despite the clear sexual connotation of the verb "to know" (*yad'a*) and its signification of her wish to consummate sexual desire, she does not need to embellish herself to bring back some of her former beauty or seduce him with her allure and be reassured of his love. Her confidence in their immediate recognition is confirmed in the meeting with R. Akiva and in his response to his disciples, in strong contrast with the encounter with Ben Kalba Savu'a, who does not recognize R. Akiva. This is an additional way of showing that the conjugal relationship—particularly in the sacrificial and extreme version presented here—is favored over the father-daughter relationship.

Interestingly, the encounter between R. Akiva and Ben Kalba Savu'a is described in terms almost identical to those used to describe the reunion of R. Akiva and his wife—both include a fall on the face and the kissing of feet. This formulation sets up R. Akiva's wife as someone who will have followers (her father and, later, her daughter, as we will see shortly)—in a kind of dual reversal of "the actions of fathers are signs to their sons" (*ma 'aseh avot siman le-banim*) into "the actions of daughters are signs to their fathers." Thus not only does R. Akiva have disciples and followers but so does his wife. By contrast, in line with Eve Kosofsky Sedgwick's view about the vital function of women in maintaining the relationships between dominant men on a homosocial continuum,[12] the overlapping attitudes of the wife and of her father toward R. Akiva depict the tie between the two men as a relationship of desire, wherein the woman functions as a communication channel mediating between two men in their shift from rivalry to love. (This recalls the role R. Yannai's daughter played in the relationship between R. Yannai and his son-in-law Judah in the second story in the series.) The pinnacle of this shift is the economic gain and the son-in-law's inclusion in the material wealth of the father, Ben Kalba Savu'a. Thus the benefits the daughter had been deprived of are now ceremonially transferred to R. Akiva and attest to the strong alliance between the two men.

The story ends with a brief description of the daughter of R. Akiva and his wife who, according to the course of the story, was probably born after R. Akiva's return from his years of study:[13] "R. Akiva's daughter did the same to Ben Azzai. And on this people say, 'Ewe follows ewe—like mother, like daughter.'"[14] Unexpectedly, the story does not end with the seemingly romantic union of R. Akiva and his wife but goes on to describe the actions of the daughter, who married Ben Azzai and, of her own will, reproduced her parents' marriage pattern. This ending of the story underscores the mother-daughter axis even more than the conjugal relationship, an axis that seemingly sidelines the father-daughter tie between Ben Kalba Savu'a and his daughter. Whereas the father-daughter relationship had been tied to the tension and the drama of dispossession and reconciliation (unsurprisingly, the reconciliation occurs between the two men rather than between the father and the daughter),[15] the mother-daughter relationship is characterized by intergenerational harmony: The mother is an example for her daughter, and the daughter hastens to behave like her. This is a "reproduction of mothering," in Nancy Chodorow's terms, meaning a reproduction of the division of labor within the family in a mode that endows gender with social and historical meaning. This social structuring perpetuates male dominance and the gender charting that identifies men with the public sphere and restricts women to the domestic realm.[16] Chodorow draws a distinction between the daughter's and the son's development. In her view the son develops by separating from the mother and by drawing away from symbiotic communication with her. By contrast the daughter builds her identity through closeness and identification with her mother and through prolonged learning of her family roles—identification and learning patterns that play a crucial role in the reproduction of the social structuring. This accentuation of the mother-daughter relationship enhances the significance of the role women/wives fulfill as promoters of their husbands' career of study while also emphasizing a legacy that perpetuates the daughters in their domestic, traditional role as those who remain behind.

A later story, probably from the late geonic period and without a parallel version in the Talmud, deals with the married life of R. Akiva's son. R. Akiva's son seemingly follows in his father's footsteps, just as in the continuance model presented by the mother and daughter:

> Another comment: "Whoso findeth a wife findeth a great good," whereas a bad wife—is there anything more bitter? A story of R. Akiva's son when he married. How did he conduct himself? After his wife entered the nuptial chamber with him, he stayed awake the whole night, reading in the Torah and studying Aggadot. He said to her: "Fetch a lamp for me and light it"; and she fetched a lamp for him and kept it lighted for him the whole night. Standing by his side, she held the light for him. He opened the scroll, and he unrolled it from beginning to end, and from end to beginning, and all night she remained standing, holding the light for him until dawn came. At dawn, R. Akiva approached his son and asked him: "Is she well-found or ill-found?" and his son replied: "She is well-found." Hence, "Whoso findeth a wife findeth a great good."[17]

Just as the daughter who married Ben Azzai continues the marital legacy she learned from her mother, so too does R. Akiva's son continue his father's legacy, favoring studying over the consummation of his sexual relationship with his wife. Like the marriage of R. Akiva and his wife, their son's marriage also embodies the model of studies taking precedence over the marital relationship. R. Akiva's son, however, adopts an improved version of it—one softer and far gentler than the one characterized by his father's prolonged absence. Here the spouses' complementary roles solve the built-in difficulty posed by the radical and extended separation of R. Akiva and his wife: The son finds a way to realize the scholarly ideal *within* the couple rather than outside it, though his preference for studying through the night when his wife enters the room appears as a clear rejection of the sexual gratification she is offering. Instead of sexual intimacy, he suggests that she should serve as his helper, assisting him in his studies by holding a lamp. The wife's role as illuminating, as shedding light on texts of wisdom, is not only practical but charged with symbolism, intimating that she is the one enabling the sage to see, learn, and understand his books; without her, he is as one who is blind and unable to engage in study. Candlelight obviously has another meaning, serving as a form of sublimation for the fire of their mutual desire, which is displaced to the Torah and transformed into a desire for learning. Sexual communication is replaced by a learning relationship, where the husband "opened the scroll, and he unrolled it from beginning to end, and from end to beginning," thereby turning her into a disciple and, in fact, a full partner in his learning.[18]

To emphasize the uniqueness of the mother-daughter relationship in the present story, we turn to another story that proposes a different tradition about the daughter's marriage. This story, in BT Shabbat, emphasizes the father-daughter drama, recounting R. Akiva's anxieties about the possibility of his daughter's marriage and her desire to separate from him to establish a separate personal and sexual identity:

> R. Akiva had a daughter.
>
> The Chaldeans [astrologers] told him, "On the very day she enters the bridal chamber, a snake will bite her, and she will die."
>
> He was greatly troubled about this. On that day, she took a brooch, stuck it into a groove, and it lodged into the eye of a serpent.
>
> The next morning, when she took it out, the snake came trailing after it.
>
> Her father said, "What did you do?"
>
> Said she, "A poor man came in the evening, knocked on the door, and everybody was busy at the banquet, so no one

heard him. I got up, took the portion you had given me, and I gave it to him."

Said he, "You have done a good deed!"

R. Akiva went out and taught: Righteousness delivers from death, and not from an unnatural death but from death itself.

BT Shabbat 156b

In this version, the possibility of the daughter's imminent marriage creates a complex setting where, as in other stories we have seen, the father and daughter appear. The presence of the other man, the groom, is not required for the development of the plot and is, to some extent, superfluous. The story does not explicate why, before his daughter's marriage, R. Akiva goes to consult the Chaldeans (astrologers), who make a horrifying prophecy: Her wedding day will also be the day of her death. Do R. Akiva's fears about the day his daughter will abandon him resonate in their prophecy, or is this perhaps an expression of his hidden wish for his daughter's death if only to prevent her move to another man? Does the father view his daughter's approaching marriage as an act of treason, whose due punishment is death by a snakebite?

According to what is described in the story, the daughter makes two symbolic moves that signal to the father that she wishes to create a sexual sphere for herself in which he has no part.[19] The first (chronologically, but second in the recounted narrative) is the symbolic transfer of the food portion her father gave her, which she gives to another man, a needy beggar standing at her doorstep. Ruhama Weiss notes that, in rabbinic parlance, food is often a sublimated representation of sexual wishes.[20] The transfer of the portion she received from her father to another man standing at her doorstep, whose voice only she hears, can therefore attest to a transfer of the father's sexual wish to another man, one with whom she can consummate her sexuality.[21] In the second move, she kills the snake that is lurking in the wall by sticking a pin in its eye. The snake, drawn from a hole in the wall, suggests the unraveling of a quasi-sexual mating that ended in death: the death of the forbidden temptation (like that of the snake that tempted the woman in the Garden of Eden). In this fatal mating, it is rather the daughter who is characterized by supremacy and by a "male" and active sexual power—she sticks the pin in the snake's eye, in the father's gaze, and thereby kills the control and the Oedipal temptation hidden in this gaze. According to Freud, eye-gouging is a figurative representation of castration.[22] In this sense, when gouging out the serpent's eye, the daughter castrates and destroys her father's desire for her. R. Akiva's reaction, "You have done a good deed!" conveys acceptance and resignation: Evidently he recognizes that his controlling and regimenting role has come to an end, and he must allow his daughter to consummate her match.[23] Unlike the model of the daughter copying and imitating her mother ("Ewe follows ewe"), the relationship between the father and the daughter leads to a desirable separation, which is tied to the father renouncing his desire for his daughter and to her willing transfer to another man who will occupy his place.

Let us return to the story discussed in this chapter. The presentation of the daughter as someone who consciously imitates her mother leads to a template of "eternal return," as it were, in a female family dynasty that sets up similar mating patterns: The women marry, but to some extent these marriages are imagined, since the spouses do not live together. This template of purported "eternal return"—based on a kind of female destiny whereby the daughter follows the mother—is further reinforced by the narrator's reliance on a proverb and on its cultural power to justify the daughter's action. The opening formula, "and on this people say," appears in the Babylonian Talmud many times and serves as a familiar linguistic marker preceding the appearance of a proverb, including all the literary and cultural meanings attached to it.[24] Robert Petsch notes that the purpose of a proverb appearing at the end of a story is to shift the discussion from the personal, single fate of the protagonist described in the plot to a general cultural claim or, in Galit Hasan-Rokem's summary of Petsch's view: "The proverb connects the unique situation . . . to the broad cultural context."[25]

In fact, the appearance of the proverb accords social recognition to the daughter's deeds and to the conjugal setting she created in her mother's wake.[26] The daughter is betrothed to Ben Azzai, who is also her father's disciple. She behaves toward him as her mother had behaved toward her father. She turns herself—to translate Boyarin's construct into female terms—into a "married nun," or perhaps it is better to define her, as does the story, as a "living widow."[27] At the same time the proverb strengthens R. Akiva's wife's standing as a kind of leader. Whereas the term "ewe" traces her relationship with R. Akiva as that between a ewe and a shepherd (as Boyarin argues), the statement "Ewe follows ewe—like mother, like daughter" makes the mother, not the father/shepherd, the one who creates a behavioral model.

From tannaitic and amoraic sources, we learn that Ben Azzai, who was probably a disciple-colleague of R. Akiva, did not want to marry and raise a family and preferred to live like an actual monk, devoting his entire life to Torah study. We thus find that, in Tosefta Yevamot, Ben Azzai made a statement of principle on the importance of procreation, which is then contrasted with the fact that he himself refrained from it:

> R. Akiva says, "Whoever sheds blood is as though he has denied the divine image since it is said, 'Whoever sheds the blood of man, by man shall his blood be shed.'" R. Eleazar b.

> Azariah says, "Whoever does not engage in procreation is as though he sheds blood and denies the divine image, for it is said, 'God made man in his own image,' and it is said, 'And you, be fruitful and multiply, etc.'" [Ben Azzai says, "Whoever does not engage in procreation is as though he sheds blood and denies the divine image, for it is said, 'God made man in his own image,' and it is said, 'And you, be fruitful and multiply, etc.'"]. R. Eleazar b. Azariah said to him, "Ben Azzai, it is well to preach when it leads to action. Some preach well and do not act well, some act well and do not preach well. Ben Azzai preaches well but does not act well." Said Ben Azzai, "What shall I do and my soul craves for Torah. Let the world be sustained by others."[28]
>
> Tosefta Yevamot 8:30

The Ketubot story, then, presents a series of characters who are all typified by the excess and exaggeration they endorse when realizing their wishes, including the price they are prepared to pay as a result. All the characters go far beyond what could be perceived as reasoned and balanced measures in their actions and choices: Ben Kalba Savu'a, who vows to disinherit his daughter; R. Akiva's wife, who sends him far away for such a long time before experiencing even a taste of a shared life with him; R. Akiva, who returns to the study house for twelve more years immediately after hearing that this is his wife's will and even before meeting with her again;[29] and again Ben Kalba Savu'a, who issues a stormy response following his renewed acquaintance with his son-in-law. This chain of intemperate deeds ends with the daughter's reproduction of her mother's legacy of waiting, and with Ben Azzai's attitude toward Torah, so intense that, in his way of life, he contradicts the values that he preaches. (He "preaches well but does not act well.")

As the craving (for studying) is exaggerated, so are the asceticism, the renunciation, and the waiting (of both mother and daughter) brought to extremes.

And yet what seems like a theme of exaggeration is actually structured in a tight template of duplication, splitting, and copying: R. Akiva's period of study is duplicated, and so is the number of his disciples. Ben Kalba Savu'a replicates his daughter's reception, splits his wealth into two halves, and gives one of them to his son-in-law. The daughter replicates her parents' lifestyle in her marriage to Ben Azzai, her father's disciple (who yearns for Torah more than he yearns for a woman and for the procreation commandment). The mother-daughter pair reproduces, as in a mirror image, the teacher-disciple pair embodied in the tie between R. Akiva and Ben Azzai. It appears that the formal duplications seek to compensate for the loss of a real and continuous relationship over many long years. Furthermore, this template of duplication and reproduction highlights not only the ridges in the construction of the story and its distance from reality but also its placement as a kind of paragon characterized by a structured order and reflecting a deep cultural logic. The tight structure, which gave form to the excess and exaggeration of the passion and the asceticism (perhaps in contrast to the excess that breaks and shatters the form, as hinted in the story of Rav Rehumi and his tragic ending), emphasizes in particular the theme of intergenerational transmission—the creation of a learning sequence in both the male and female dynasties, as well as the way they intersect.

THE SEVENTH STORY

Rava and His Son Rav Yosef

The last story in the series, in contrast to most of the preceding ones (but resembling the third story, about Rabbi and his son, who marries R. Jose b. Zimra's daughter), presents a scholar who wishes to interrupt his long absence for a brief family visit.[1] In this story, the father rejects the initiative, representing a male stance that supports long absences and clearly favors Torah study over the conjugal and family interest, and over the husband's intimate relations with his wife. The father is seemingly furious about the independent choice of his son who, after all, is merely heeding an ancient command ("therefore a man leaves his father and his mother and cleaves to his wife, and they become one flesh" [Gen. 2:24]). The father is even willing, if necessary, to unhesitatingly resort to violence in order to strengthen his authority and his position as head of the family hierarchy: He "took up a tool, and went out to meet him," as one who goes out to a duel. This is not only a face-to-face battle between a father and his son, an Oedipal struggle over individuation and separation.[2] More than anything, this is a battle between clashing and contradictory positions: between one who remembers the importance of conjugal and family ties, the needs of his wife, as well as his own need to see her, and another who belittles their importance vis-à-vis the duty of Torah study and assumes the role of the symbolic father in charge of law, duty, authority, and the spirit.

The linguistic ambiguity between "your whore" (*zonatkha*) and "your dove" (*yonatkha*) in reference to the son's spouse further attests to the woman's debased status when compared to devotion to study. Both terms are perceived as humiliating insults that send father and son into a prolonged quarrel. The linguistic proximity between the two Hebrew words attests to their conceptual proximity: In the third story in the series, R. Judah ha-Nasi marries off his son to R. Jose b. Zimra's daughter, who in the course of her husband's prolonged absence becomes barren. Rabbi fears that, were his son to marry yet another woman, "it will be said, this one is his wife and that one his whore." The very perception of the woman as attractive and desirable to her husband, who wished to stay with her even at the expense of his Torah study—marks the woman as a whore. And as in the story about Rav Rehumi's wife that opened the discussion of the chain of stories, heterosexual love and desire are indirectly marked as dubious realms, at times even as dangers to be kept out and excluded. The "dove" (*yonah*)—the beloved—is a whore (*zonah*) whose sexuality threatens the male institution of Torah study.[3] The same is true here: Missing his wife and actually coming to visit her mark the son as a weakling of whom his father is ashamed; that is, as one who will eventually be incapable of fulfilling the fatherly role, which requires being able to negate fleeting emotional and physical dimensions and emphasize spiritual and abstract ones instead. The son, who does not show restraint, thereby becomes an equal of the inferior woman—hence his affront and his quarrel.

Particularly interesting is the choice to locate this story at the end of the series. The first in this chain of stories, about Rav Rehumi and his wife, also takes place on the eve of Yom Kippur. In both stories the day is tied to sexuality and to violence. Their shared timing strengthens the impression of a "frame" and a planned structure for this chain of stories, tying together the first and last ones in additional ways. Both stories lead to an event conveying a powerful emotional experience—the tear of Rav Rehumi's wife in the first story and the father-son quarrel in the last one. These external manifestations of mental events are atypical in talmudic stories, which tend to report actions that attest indirectly to developments in the protagonist's psyche. The fundamental difference between the positions of Rav Rehumi and his wife, which are located along the high-low axis, versus the horizontal confrontation between the father and the son in the last story, is also a point of interest. Indeed the first stories in the chain present attitudes located along the high-low axis, such as the roof versus the ground and the fall from the roof to the ground in the first story, about Rav Rehumi; R. Yannai's ascent to a high place to gain a better view of the expected return of Judah, his son-in-law, in the second story; and the concern with status lineages around the marriage of Rabbi's son in the third story. But the next stories in the chain highlight the parties' horizontal movement vis-à-vis one another. The last story, where the rival sides—father versus son—confront one another and take up tools, points to increased intergenerational tension and its radicalization into violence.

Yom Kippur is an extreme time of decisions, which sharpens the differences between spheres, times, and ideas. But this story—and in fact the entire sequence of stories—ends on a note of indecision: Father and son are so immersed in their quarrel that they do not even find time for the last meal before the fast, which clearly demarcates the border between sacred and profane. Ultimately, we do not know which one of them was defeated and which of the attitudes won out—the one that favors the conjugal and family union or the one that upholds prolonged absences for the purpose of studying Torah.

Finishing the series with a story that ends badly and inconclusively posed a challenge to the scholars who dealt with it. Yona Fraenkel chose to ignore the last story and ended his discussion on an optimistic note, with the story of R. Akiva and his wife, which, as noted, appears to him as a positive account of harmonious couplehood.[4] Daniel Boyarin dealt with the story briefly and defined it as "one of the most appalling stories of a Rabbi's behavior in the Talmud."[5] He claims that closing the chain with this story actually reflects the intensity of the conflict evoked by the Babylonian practice of married monks—sages who left to study Torah for many years and did not visit their families.[6]

Along the lines of Boyarin's claim, we hold that the location of the last story in the sequence makes it harder to determine the rabbinic stance on this question, which at the end of the discussion apparently remains unsettled. Following precisely after the R. Akiva story, which seemingly provides a fanciful-ideal solution to the conflict as the wife consents to, and even participates in, the prolonged absence, the last story clarifies that there is no resolution. The father-son quarrel on the eve of the Day of Judgment is emblematic of the clash between the contradictory positions, and the choice to end the series with this clash attests, more than anything, to a narrative choice to leave the question open.

If we return the focus to the father's tie to his children, however, we cannot ignore that, even if the issue of absence from home remains unresolved, insofar as the relationships within the family are concerned, the decision to end the series with this story leaves a bad taste regarding the father-son relationship. Here we find a fundamental reversal of the picture reflected in the previous story, which described a legacy and its conciliatory and almost harmonious reproductive transmission, including the study and imitation patterns set by R. Akiva and his wife. The welcome R. Akiva encountered is the diametrical opposite of the harsh and violent reception of Rav Yosef by Rava, his father, and the chain of stories ends by depicting the father-son relationship as a rivalry and struggle rather than a warm and harmonious bond.

Quantitatively, in the chain of stories more decisive weight is granted to those accounts where the father-son (or father-daughter) relationships emerge as tense and not ideal. One story in the entire series—the story of R. Hama b. Bisa and R. Oshayah—describes harmonious relationships between the generations without alienation, envy, or harsh consequences despite (and in fact because of) the prolonged absence for study purposes. Even the story of R. Akiva and his wife—which, as we have shown, led to a harmonious reconciliation between the generations and to the dynastic continuity of both the father and the mother—entails a serious conflict between Ben Kalba Savu'a and his daughter, which led to her exclusion and dispossession. Ending the chain with a story about a violent struggle between a father and his son continues to depict absence in a negative light and shows the damage it inflicts on the family structure—not only to the husband-wife relationship but also, and mainly, to the crucial and constitutive relationship between a father and his children.

EPILOGUE

In this book we offer an outline for a renewed discussion of the chain of stories in tractate Ketubot, changing the perspective by shifting the spotlight from the couple to another family drama: one focused on the relationship between the present-absent father and his children. This shift exposes a carefully organized literary sequence that presents the sages' diverse views on their expectations from their sons and daughters and the awareness of the high price they demand. In our reading of the stories, we discussed the types of family tensions they reflect: the conjugal tension, the tension between father and daughter, and the tension between father and son. The broader family context exposes, in our view, the complexity of the relationships between the father and his children—sons and daughters—along the axis between presence and absence, complicating the tension between the mundane domestic sphere and the spiritual-learning sphere of the *beth midrash*. Besides the texts' concern with the place of the daughter in the family—itself rare in rabbinic literature—our reading reveals the exclusion from the stories of the woman's place, or of women's interests, even when they seem to be attended to. Our reading fills a certain gap that stems from the scant rabbinic concern with the place and role of the father within the domestic sphere, and sheds some light on the shadowed areas tied to his character and to his seemingly absolute control over the members of his household.

While previous readings of this chain of stories stressed the gaps and the conflicting demands posed in each of the contradictory spheres—the woman/the home versus the *beth midrash*—our reading model makes this binary tension more complex. Introducing the children into the picture—and the questions about their identity, their upbringing, and the hopes of continuity embodied by them—blunts the dichotomy counterposing the home as a mundane and material, female sphere against the *beth midrash* as a sphere of spirit and knowledge. Addressing the place of sons and daughters in the general family picture, in addition to the conjugal role, attests that the family elements encroach on the study sphere just as the spiritual needs find expression in the domestic sphere. Moreover, the concepts of absence and presence seem more complex than what they appear at first glance: The father's absence is also a form of presence and accompaniment (as in the story of R. Hama), while his return/presence is largely a continuation of his absence and disappearance (as in the R. Yannai story). Thus attention to the father's relationship with his sons and daughters, besides his relationship with his wife, clears the way for a view of the sage not merely as someone in tension with his spouse but also as someone whose very status, power, and authority, which are derived from his paternal role, are reexamined through the issues that emerge in the stories.

We wish to briefly discuss it a short story by S. Y. Agnon, "At the Outset of the Day," because the family tie at its center, between a father and his daughter, serves as an axis that also mediates the relationship with the *beth midrash*. The story creates a complex structure of relationships between the family approach and the religious-spiritual approach to the realms of holiness, ritual, and study. This structure is also dominant in the chain of stories we have read and interpreted in this book which, like the Agnon story, opens and closes at a symbolic and dramatic time—the eve of Yom Kippur.

"At the Outset of the Day" (*'Im Kenissat ha-Yom*)[1] tells the story of a father who, with his young daughter, hurriedly flees his home to escape from brutal attackers on the eve of Yom Kippur. He returns, destitute, to the city where he grew up. At the outset of the holy day, they enter the city's Great Synagogue, which has two houses of study, an old one and an adjacent new one. At the synagogue, the father promises his daughter: "Good men will come at once and give me a tallit with an adornment of silver just like the one the enemy tore. . . . You, my darling, they will bring a little prayer book full of letters, full of all of the letters of the alphabet and the vowel marks, too" (371). This analogy between the clothing and the book, between text and textile, continues throughout this enigmatic story, which is built as a nightmare. While he speaks, the little girl's clothes go up in flames, set on fire by a memorial candle that had been lit in the gallery. The father rips off the burning garment and tries to find something with which to cover his daughter. He finds no cover in the synagogue, not even in the *genizah* corner, where torn holy books are kept: "When books were read, they were rent; but now that books are not read, they are not rent" (372). He hurries to the home of R. Alter, the *mohel*, who had also been the narrator's *mohel*, but finds no clothes there for his daughter, since everyone is as poor as he is, and their garments are also torn. On returning to the synagogue, he finds his daughter naked and shivering from cold: "I found her standing in a corner of the courtyard pressed against the wall next to the purification board on which the dead are washed. Her hair was loose and wrapped about her" (374). The father hugs her to keep her warm, and the men who enter the synagogue see them and mock him, provoking his anger. His daughter wants them to run away, but he manages to calm her down by describing to her the sight of the old *beth midrash* and of the Torah scroll wrapped in a splendid mantle, protected by a rope, and kept in its place. At the end of the short story, the father prays devotedly, and the sleepy, naked daughter repeats his melodies in her sleep.[2]

Scholars who have dealt with this story have emphasized, from various directions, its allegorical dimension.[3] Samuel Leiter and Rachel Ofer point to the daughter-soul connection and describe the father as one yearning to return the soul to its ancient, pure state, which the young naked daughter in a way symbolizes.[4] Baruch Kurzweil, by contrast, sees in the daughter a representation of modernity's confusion as it confronts the perfect and harmonious traditional past: "The candle, which is a remembrance of what was, is actually the cause of the fire. The girl of the new generation is left naked, daughter of a cruel reality without a God. Only he, the narrator alone, a member of the old generation, is still dressed."[5]

Yet the narrator describes the father's search for cover for his daughter as a failure, given that the holy texts, which he wanted to use to clothe the naked girl, had long been torn and abandoned. Holiness was no longer found there; only emptiness and spiritual poverty remained. The story thus conveys the desire to meld the daughter—who is perceived as a pure, mindless, and innocent infant—with the sources (including textual, personal, and spiritual ones).[6] Agnon himself offers a puzzling interpretation of the little girl as a symbol: "At times she takes the form of an old woman and at times the form of a little girl. And when she takes the form of a little girl, don't imagine that your soul is as pure as a little girl; this is but an indication that she passionately yearns to recapture the purity of her infancy when she was free of sin. The fool substitutes the *form* for the *need*; the wise man substitutes *will* for *need*" (375, emphasis in original). This passage suggests that part of the story's allegorical dimension deals also with the very nature of allegorical interpretation (a kind of midrash), one that entails the replacement of an overt layer by a covert one. Agnon intimates in this passage that, on the way from the overt to the covert, interpretive mistakes occasionally occur, and the reference to an infant free of sin is understood as a characterization of the soul instead of a characterization of the very desire to be purified and the actual craving for the Torah. Elsewhere in the story he notes that this matter "is by no means allegorical but a simple and straightforward affair" (376).

The desire that the covert layer strives for, the desire for Torah, which is concretized in the illuminated vision of the old *beth midrash*, is expressed in the abandonment of the naked young girl in the overt layer of the story, the "simple and straightforward" one. The various interpretations given to this story, as noted, preferred to discuss the signified, conveniently avoiding the troublesome signifier. Indeed, by contrast with the talmudic stories in the chain we read, here a father and his daughter appear in the same sphere. He does not turn to his own affairs but seeks to protect her, and the connection between them is touching. It is hard, however, not to wonder at the father's strange behavior: a father who neglects his daughter and proves so incompetent at protecting her safety, defending her honor, and preserving her body heat—a father who searches for torn page scraps in the *genizah* and leaves her behind, naked, while he turns to his neighbors without ever considering taking off his own shirt to cover the body of his child. Thus while the story tempts us to interpret its material elements as spiritual ones, the allegorical act itself enables us to ignore the overt layer. Like an open letter, this overt layer tells another story of desire—a transgressive story bringing incestuous desire into the holy of holies at that liminal period of the eve of Yom Kippur that invites licentiousness and chaos prior to the affliction that will purify the soul.[7] The interpretation of the symbols does not close the gaps that open up following the puzzling choices of the father who, as the narrator describes him, is busy with the substitution of "will for need."

The story seriously undermines the resilience and stability of the father figure who, just as he had been unable to protect his home from the invading enemy, fails to protect his daughter from the fire or to provide her with clothes when she is shivering from the cold. The father knew how to clothe the scroll that had been written "in memory of the souls of days that had departed" (377), with a "red mantle with silver points" (377), which is described as a splendid gown but at the same time as a kind of coat for the child. His daughter, in contrast to the protected and magnificent Torah scroll, is forced to cover her body with her own hair, as if she knew that the chain of learning and support—from father to daughter—had been broken, and she must now fulfill her needs by herself.

The daughter's act of covering herself with her hair, possibly to keep her body warm and possibly to hide it, evokes the rabbinic narrative tradition about the daughter of Nakdimon b. Gorion, who came from a rich family that lost its wealth during the revolt and the destruction of the Temple. In her meeting with Rabban Yohanan b. Zakkai (which also reveals direct and indirect characteristics of a father-daughter encounter), she covers herself with her hair:

It once happened that while Rabban Johanan ben Zakkai was riding an ass and his disciples were following him, he saw a young woman gathering barley grains from under the feet of Arab cattle.

When she saw Rabban Johanan ben Zakkai, she covered her face with her hair, stood up before him, and said to him, "Master, grant me sustenance."

He asked her, "Whose daughter are you?"

She replied, "I am the daughter of Nakdimon ben Gorion." "Master," she continued, "you no doubt remember when you signed my marriage contract [*Ketubah*]."

Rabban Johanan ben Zakkai then said to his disciples, "I did indeed sign this woman's marriage contract, and I noticed in it a stipulation of one million gold denar payable to her by her father-in-law's family and her own family.

"Whenever they went to worship at the Temple Mount, fine woolen carpets were spread out for them to walk on, and they would enter, prostrate themselves, and return joyfully to their homes. All my life I wondered about the meaning of the verse, 'If thou know not, O thou fairest among women, go thy way forth by the footsteps of the flock, and feed thy kids beside the shepherds' tents' (Song 1:8), but now I found it—read not *gediyotayik* ['your kids'] but *gewiyotayik* ['your bodies']. As long as Israel do the will of God, no nation or kingdom can rule over them, but when Israel do not do God's will, He delivers them into the hand of the lowliest of nations, and not only into the hands of the lowliest of nations but also under the feet of the cattle of the lowliest of nations."

Sifre Deuteronomy[8]

Like this story, Agnon's story also deals with a harsh loss of assets and status—both in the economic, material sense and in the spiritual sense—and with the precipitous decline of the light, the plenitude, and the love of Torah of days past to abject and degrading poverty. The fall is concretized in the change of cover—from a delicate and expensive fabric spread under the feet (or the girl's "lovely clothes" in Agnon's story) into the hair that serves to cover the body, given the destitute girl's lack of any clothing. In both stories the "textile" hints to a "text," creating an opportunity to interpret the text's meaning. The meeting with the woman leads Rabban Yohanan b. Zakkai to a radical interpretation of a verse from Song of Songs, which fits the situation of the people of Israel after the destruction of the Temple. Similarly, the father in Agnon's story engages in textual interpretation and views the naked child as a symbol conveying a purification wish. The connection between the two stories could also indicate that, like Yohanan b. Zakkai, Agnon, too, sees the material decline as punishment for spiritual decline (and this too by hinting at Song of Songs: "I sought but found nothing. Wherever I directed by eyes, I met emptiness" [372]).[9]

What we view as the prominent issue here is, in both cases, the abandonment of the wretched daughter—by Yohanan b. Zakkai, who does not answer her call ("grant me sustenance"), and by the father, who fails to find cover for his naked child. Resonating sharply in the father's failure is obviously the wearing away of the supreme father who, as defined by Agnon, is "our Father in heaven, who is my father and your father and the father of the whole world" (372). Here the story intimates that interpretation cannot close gaps or truly meet physical and spiritual needs (such as, for example, the need for meaning). The wise man who substitutes "will for need" neglects the physical reality of the need—a reality of nakedness, poverty, and cold—in favor of spiritual and hermeneutical lessons.

We chose to mention Agnon's story in our epilogue because he emphasizes the place and role of the father at both the symbolic and realistic levels: The father represents the attraction of the *beth midrash* and of textual and spiritual sources, yet he is also entrusted with the welfare and safety of his children. In the story "At the Outset of the Day," the father appears to be a failure on both counts, while the poor, naked daughter is the one who experiences a dimension of revelation, albeit one entailing a forbidden transgression that was transformed into a desire for Torah and prayer.

When dealing with Agnon's story, scholars preferred to ignore the troubling aspects of family ties and marginalize their importance, favoring instead discussions of the symbolic level, which deserves to be interpreted but is also easier to accept and contain. We see a similar phenomenon in the interpretations thus far given to the chain of stories from BT Ketubot, which examine the loaded space created between the father and his children on the one hand and the *beth midrash* on the other. These interpretations preferred to emphasize the tension between the conjugal desire and the scholarly desire as the driving force in the stories; yet there is in them an additional significant layer that is both loaded and repressed, touching on the father figure and his presence in the family relationship. As in Agnon's story, concrete expressions of fatherhood are evident as presence, care, protection, identification, or, in their absence, as distance, detachment, jealousy, competitiveness, violence, and abandonment. Precisely these expressions, found beside and within the long chain of interpretation, study, and Midrash, may reveal other aspects of the narrative tradition, other stories, bringing back a different fatherhood from its prolonged absence.

NOTES

PREFACE

1. Yona Fraenkel, *Studies on the Spiritual World of the Aggadic Story* (in Hebrew) (Tel Aviv: Hakibbutz Hameuchad, 1981); Shulamit Valler, *Women and Womanhood in the Talmud*, trans. Betty Sigler Rozen (Providence, RI: Brown University, 1999); Tal Ilan, *Mine and Yours Are Hers: Retrieving Women's History from Rabbinic Literature* (Leiden: Brill, 1997); Daniel Boyarin, *Carnal Israel: Reading Sex in Talmudic Culture* (Berkeley: University of California Press, 1993); Jeffrey L. Rubenstein, *The Culture of the Babylonian Talmud* (Baltimore, MD: Johns Hopkins University Press, 2003), 102–122. Further studies offering readings of some of the units in this chain of stories will be mentioned as necessary.
2. This book does not attempt to present a broad or comprehensive picture of the actual figure of the father in rabbinic culture. Our aim is to examine the cultural and literary images that appear only in one narrative setting and to trace the contours of the father figure that emerges from it. Researchers dealing with the figure of the father within the family structure in rabbinic culture or in late antiquity will, so we hope, find the present discussion useful.

3. This is not the place to enter into a broad discussion on the editing of story sequences in the Babylonian Talmud. Following previous studies, Joshua Levinson ascribes significance to the editing endeavor and claims that the groups of the stories in the Babylonian Talmud can be viewed as "an independent literary unit, with a frame or an organizing principle of its own . . . built from several separate units." See Joshua Levinson, *The Twice-Told Tale: A Poetics of the Exegetical Narrative in Rabbinic Midrash* (in Hebrew) (Jerusalem: Magnes, 2005), 280, and references there. For a description of narrative sequences in the Babylonian Talmud, see Eli Yassif, "The Cycle of Tales in Rabbinic Literature" (in Hebrew), *Jerusalem Studies in Hebrew Literature* 12 (1990):103–145.
4. Dina Stein, "Collapsing Structures: Discourse and the Destruction of the Temple in the Babylonian Talmud," *Jewish Quarterly Review* 98, no. 1 (2008): 7.
5. At times he uses this term alternatively with that of "open closure."
6. Itay Marienberg-Milikowsky, "'Beyond the Matter': Stories and Their Contexts in the Babylonian Talmud—Repeated Stories as a Test Case" (in Hebrew) (PhD diss., Ben-Gurion University of the Negev, 2015), 54. Emphasis in the original.
7. Even without explicitly stating this, our approach engages in a complex dialogue with the hermeneutical stance of Yona Fraenkel, who adopted the absolute "closure" of the individual story, with all the historical and literary implications that follow, as the key assumption of his research. For a summary of his view, see, for example, Yona Fraenkel, "Hermeneutic Problems in the Study of the Aggadic Narrative" (in Hebrew), *Tarbiz* 47 (1978): 107–256; idem, *Studies on the Spiritual World*, 32–50. For a detailed review of his approach and of the wide scholarly reactions to it, see Joshua Levinson, "From Parable to Invention: The Growth of Fiction as a Cultural Category" (in Hebrew), in *Higayon l'Yona: New Aspects in the Study of Midrash, Aggadah, and Piyut in Honor of Professor Yona Fraenkel*, ed. Joshua Levinson, Jacob Elbaum, Galit Hasan-Rokem (Jerusalem: Magnes Press, 2006); Marienberg-Milikowsky, "Beyond the Matter," 40–44.
8. See, for example, her opening statement in her study on Lamentations Rabba: "Scholars addressing folk narrative deal with the multilayered

and heterogeneous origins of the authority articulated in rabbinic Aggadah. They thereby point to a distinctive source for a crucial stylistic and structural feature of this literature, its tendency to convey complex meanings through multivocal modes of discourse." Galit Hasan-Rokem, *Web of Life: Folklore and Midrash in Rabbinic Literature,* trans. Batya Stein (Stanford, CA: Stanford University Press, 2000), 7. Also in this spirit, see the opening of her book on neighbors' stories, *Tales of the Neighborhood: Jewish Narrative Dialogues in Late Antiquity* (Berkeley: University of California Press, 2003), 1–2.

THE CHAIN OF STORIES

1. In both MS Munich and MS Petersburg 187, the addition "and he did not come" appears, emphasizing the husband's absence and his unwillingness to abandon his studies.
2. In MS Munich 95, MS Petersburg 187, MS Vatican 113, MS Vatican 487.11, the third-person singular, "he saw," is replaced by a plural, "they saw," which is a significant change—everyone, not only R. Yannai, saw the pillar of fire.
3. In MS Petersburg 187, an addition appears here claiming that the marriage was not consummated. This intervention borders on the parodic and the grotesque by denoting the obvious—after the bride died, there was no marriage. This addition illustrates the violence surrounding the entire story, which relies to a large extent on the significance ascribed to patriarchal dynasties, a significance that makes it possible to kill a woman meant to move from one dynasty to another.
4. In MS Petersburg 187, MS Vatican 130, and in MS Vatican 11.487, an addition appears here clarifying that the death was caused by the status gap between the families.
5. In MS Petersburg 187, an addition appears here: "Now I do not know whether this or that is better." This surprising addition strengthens the reflective dimension in the father's response. He does not know which of the two ways is preferable: going away from home to study Torah or remaining in the domestic space and sharing in the process of raising and educating the children.

6. In MS Munich 97 and in MS Petersburg 187, the general term "his son" is replaced by the word *yanuka* (baby or child). This term emphasizes the gap between the mother's and the father's perceptions—whereas the father thinks of his son (whom he does not recognize) as a scholar, his wife sees him as their young child and therefore fails to understand why the father would rise up before him.
7. A gender change features in MS Petersburg 187—the speaker is an old woman. This is an interesting and significant change that turns the nasty remark that appears in the printed version into an intra-gender discussion of principle between two women—an older woman who criticizes a younger one for her willingness to sacrifice her life. By contrast, in MS Vatican 113, the word *saba* (old man) is replaced by the word *gavra* (man).
8. In the original Aramaic –*mana*, which could also be rendered as weapon.
9. A different, more violent, version of the encounter appears in MS Petersburg 187, where the father is described as "injuring his son in the head" and pursuing him with an axe.

INTRODUCTION

1. Ursula Owen, *Fathers: Reflections by Daughters* (New York: Pantheon Books, 1985), xii.
2. Galit Hasan-Rokem, *Web of Life: Folklore and Midrash in Rabbinic Literature*, trans. Batya Stein (Stanford, CA: Stanford University Press, 2000), 109; idem, *Tales of the Neighborhood: Jewish Narrative Dialogues in Late Antiquity* (Berkeley: University of California Press, 2003), 32.
3. See Adiel Schremer, *Male and Female He Created Them: Jewish Marriage in the Late Second Temple, Mishnah, and Talmud Periods* (in Hebrew) (Jerusalem: Zalman Shazar Center for Jewish History, 2003), 35, and references there. On the father's dominant role and his quest for intellectual parenthood, see, for example, Daniel Boyarin, *Carnal Israel: Reading Sex in Talmudic Culture* (Berkeley: University of California Press, 1993), 134–166; Dina Stein, *Maxims, Magic, Myth: A Folkloristic Perspective of Pirkei deRabbi Eliezer* (in Hebrew) (Jerusalem: Magnes

Press, 2004); Haim Weiss, "Worthless Son of Worthy Father? Political Struggles, Torah Study, and Identity in the Family of R. Simon Bar Yohai" (in Hebrew), in *Peace and War in Jewish Culture,* ed. Avriel Bar-Levav (Jerusalem: Zalman Shazar Center for Jewish History, 2006), 67–83 and references in these articles.

4. For an extensive discussion of female identity, domestic space, and neighbors' relations, and on the complexity of defining the border between them in rabbinic literature, see Hasan-Rokem, *Tales of the Neighborhood.*
5. Yona Fraenkel, *Studies on the Spiritual World of the Aggadic Story* (in Hebrew) (Tel Aviv: Hakibbutz Hameuchad, 1981), 99–115. Note that, rather unusually, Fraenkel went beyond the individual story and related to this entire literary complex as one whole, even viewing it as "one of the most beautiful collections of stories in the whole of Aggadic literature" (100). See also Shulamit Valler, *Women and Womanhood in the Talmud,* trans. Betty Sigler Rozen (Providence, RI: Brown University, 1999), 51–76; Tal Ilan, *Mine and Yours Are Hers: Retrieving Women's History from Rabbinic Literature* (Leiden: Brill, 1997), 207–215; Jeffrey L. Rubenstein, *The Culture of the Babylonian Talmud* (Baltimore, MD: Johns Hopkins University Press, 2003), 102–122. For a discussion of some of the stories in this unit, see Jeffrey Rubenstein, *Rabbinic Stories* (New York: Paulist Press, 2002), 139–145; Dina Stein, "Collapsing Structures: Discourse and the Destruction of the Temple in the Babylonian Talmud," *Jewish Quarterly Review* 98, no. 1 (2008): 1–28.
6. Both Ilan and Rubenstein single out for discussion the difference between Babylonia and the Land of Israel regarding the length of the sages' absence from home and the legitimacy of this absence.
7. Stein, "Collapsing Structures," 5. See also Oded Israeli, "*Kiddushin,* Marriage, and Torah Study in the Stories of R. Akiva and the Daughter of Kalba Savu'a" (in Hebrew), *Assufot: Journal on Aggadah and Midrash* 1 (2010–2011): 94–104.
8. M. Ketubot 5:6.
9. M. Ketubot 5:5, 7. M. Ketubot 5:7 deals also with the rebellious husband (who refuses to have intercourse with his wife), though here, too, emphasizing the gap between men and women. As opposed to the

rebellious wife, whose *ketubah* is reduced by seven *denars*, a rebellious husband adds only three *denars* to his wife's *ketubah*.

10. This almost enigmatic formulation relates to a man who supports his wife through a guardian or an emissary, and the question discussed in this mishnah is the amount the missing husband is required to give to his wife through that emissary. See M. Ketubot 5:8.
11. As Schremer shows, sexual fulfillment with one's wife is meant not for her pleasure but, above all, to save the husband from sin, meaning to prevent him from satisfying his lust in illegal or illegitimate ways. See Schremer, *Male and Female*, 308–310, and his many references there.
12. M. Yoma 1:1.
13. Cynthia Baker, *Rebuilding the House of Israel: Architectures of Gender in Jewish Antiquity* (Stanford, CA: Stanford University Press, 2002), explores the relationship between female and spatial images and expands this claim to the point of absolute identification between the woman and the house: "in a number of rabbinic constructions, a house is not *where* a woman/wife is, but rather a house is, in part, *who* and *what* she is" (35, emphasis in the original). Beside this claim, which enhances the woman-home identification, Baker considers the appearance of inside and outside at the architectural level: the home space versus the public space. She suggests an interesting argument: Counterintuitively, these spaces encroached on one another so that the limits on the movement and transition between them were fluid rather than rigid. For a claim in this spirit, see Hasan-Rokem, *Tales of the Neighborhood*, 18, and specifically referring to Baker, see ibid., 30, 67. Charlotte Elisheva Fonrobert, *Menstrual Purity: Rabbinic and Christian Reconstructions of Biblical Gender* (Stanford, CA: Stanford University Press, 2000), in her comprehensive study of menstrual blood in rabbinic literature, emphasizes the sages' broad use of architectural metaphors when discussing female anatomy. She shows that, to describe the various sources of blood, they built complex architectural structures that included houses, rooms, attics, and passages. See ibid., 40–67.
14. Leviticus Rabba is a midrash from the Land of Israel, and our discussion focuses on a Babylonian chain of stories. Nevertheless we hold that, despite the gaps between the Land of Israel and Babylonia in all

that concerns the approach to conjugal relationships and sexuality, this midrash illustrates the tension in rabbinic literature regarding women's movement from the home and back, and that is why we chose to consider it here. Furthermore, in the Babylonian Talmud, too, we find a puzzling and unexplained description of a husband requiring his wife to spit on a scholar, here involving R. Shimon b. Gamaliel: "A man who said to his wife, '*Konam* [I swear] that you do not benefit from me until you spit on R. Shimon b. Gamaliel.' She went and spat on his garment" (BT Nedarim 66b). R. Shimon b. Gamaliel is indeed a *tanna* in the Land of Israel, but his presence in a Babylonian Talmud story attests that the theme itself was widespread in both places. For a brief discussion of this source, see Shulamit Valler, "Domestic Strife and Domestic Harmony in the Literature of the Sages" (in Hebrew), in *Peace and War in Jewish Culture*, ed. Bar-Levav, 18.

15. For this version, see Boyarin, *Carnal Israel*, 187. An additional parallel version appears in PT Sotah 1:4, and see the discussion of it in Valler, "Domestic Strife and Domestic Harmony." For other studies that dealt with this story, see another discussion of it in Hasan-Rokem, *Tales of the Neighborhood*, 76–81; Boyarin, *Carnal Israel*, 187–189; Admiel Kosman, *Women's Tractate: Wisdom, Love, Faithfulness, Passion, Beauty, Sex, Holiness* (in Hebrew) (Jerusalem: Keter, 2007), 178–184.
16. Neighboring cultures offer evidence of the use of spitting as a medical or magical remedy. The New Testament describes Jesus' healing use of spitting in several cases. Thus we are told that Jesus cured a deaf man by spitting on his tongue (Mark 7:33), and in other cases he opened up the eyes of a blind man by spitting on his eyes (Mark 8:22–25; John 9). For a broad discussion of the magical and medical uses of spitting in the Jewish, Christian, and Muslim worlds , see Adam Collins Bursi, "Holy Spit and Magic Spells: Religion, Magic and the Body in Late Ancient Judaism, Christianity, and Islam" (PhD diss., Cornell University, 2015), and his extensive bibliography. For a specific discussion of the spitting story about R. Meir, see ibid., 44–45, 149.
17. See Galit Hasan Rokem, "The Three-Folded Cord: On Sexuality, Couplehood, and Womanhood in Rabbinic Literature" (in Hebrew), *Theory and Criticism* 7 (1995): 262.

18. Sherry B. Ortner, "Is Female to Male as Nature Is to Culture?" in *Women, Culture, and Society*, ed. Michelle Zimbalist Rosaldo, Louise Lamphere, and Joan Bamberger (Stanford, CA: Stanford University Press, 1974), 79.
19. Pierre Bourdieu, *Masculine Domination*, trans. Richard Nice (Stanford, CA: Stanford University Press, 2002).
20. Joan W. Scott, "Gender: A Useful Category of Historical Analysis," *American Historical Review* 91 (1986): 1053–1075. In this context she quotes the French anthropologist Maurice Godelier: "It is not sexuality which haunts society, but society which haunts the body's sexuality. Sex-related differences between bodies are continually summoned as testimony to social relations and phenomena that have nothing to do with sexuality. Not only as testimony to, but also testimony for—in other words, as legitimation" (1069). See Maurice Godelier, "The Origins of Male Domination," *New Left Review* 127 (May–June 1981): 17.
21. On these names as referring to later Babylonian sages, see Rubenstein, *The Culture of the Babylonian Talmud*, 105.
22. Schremer, *Male and Female*, 69. In this context see also Judith R. Baskin, *Midrashic Women: Formations of the Feminine in Rabbinic Literature* (Hanover, NH: Brandeis University Press, 2002), 103–105. We do not, as noted, wish to make a final determination on the historical circumstances. Formulations should, therefore, perhaps be slightly qualified to read that the Talmud sets an ideal whereby sages are meant to prefer studying to married life. The question whether this was indeed the case is hard to answer directly by relying on the text and is not the concern of our study.
23. See, for example, Valler, *Women and Womanhood*, 51–52: "Scrutiny of these stories and the way they are edited leads to the conclusion that the Sages were well aware of women's other hardships, particularly the spiritual ones. The editor of the collection, moreover, tried to transmit the message that permission to leave home for long periods of study depended entirely, at least morally, on the wife's feelings and wishes."
24. On this context, see Moshe Lavee, "Accepting the Other and Otherness: Highlighting and Blurring Processes in Rabbinic Literature" (in Hebrew), *Mishlav* 36 (2002): 105, and also Eli Yassif, "The Cycle of

Tales in Rabbinic Literature" (in Hebrew), *Jerusalem Studies in Hebrew Literature* 12 (1990): 133, who do hint at the possibility of reading this chain of stories from a family perspective but do not develop it.

FIRST STORY

1. Yona Fraenkel, *Studies on the Spiritual World of the Aggadic Story* (in Hebrew) (Tel Aviv: Hakibbutz Hameuchad, 1981), 101; Shulamit Valler, *Women and Womanhood in the Talmud*, trans. Betty Sigler Rozen (Providence, RI: Brown University, 1999), 74–75; Daniel Boyarin, *Carnal Israel: Reading Sex in Talmudic Culture* (Berkeley: University of California Press, 1993), 146–149. Jeffrey Rubenstein emphasizes the tension between Halakhah, which allows prolonged absences from the home, and Aggadah, which subverts the halakhic position while exposing the danger of long absences. See Jeffrey Rubenstein, *Rabbinic Stories* (New York: Paulist Press, 2002), 105. For additional readings of this story, see David Zimmerman, *Eight Love Stories from Talmud and Midrash* (in Hebrew) (Tel Aviv: Sifriat Hapoalim, 1981), 14–17; Ruth Calderon, *A Bride for One Night: Talmud Tales*, trans. Ilana Kurshan (Lincoln, NE/ Philadelphia: University of Nebraska Press/Jewish Publication Society, 2014), 31–38; Ari Elon, *Alma Di* (in Hebrew) (Tel Aviv: Miskal, 2011), 124–128.
2. The prohibition on sexual relations on Yom Kippur is first mentioned in the Mishnah in the list of acts prohibited on that day: "On Yom Kippur—eating, drinking, washing, anointing, putting on sandals, and conjugal intercourse are forbidden" (M. Yoma 8:1). The connection of this prohibition to affliction is explained in BT Yoma 77b: "Whence do we know that [abstention from] sexual intercourse is considered an affliction? Because it is written: 'If you afflict my daughters, or if you take wives besides my daughters' (Gen. 31:50)." The Genesis verse cites Laban who, when drawing a covenant with Jacob, adjures him to refrain from taking any more wives besides his daughters. Two lessons can be learned from the Gemara's choice of this verse. One is that sexual intercourse (or abstention from it, as Rashi claims *ad locum*) is an affliction, and the second—and more significant from the present perspective—is that the source the Gemara relies on

regarding the prohibition of sexual intercourse on Yom Kippur is also related to a father's supervising gaze (in this case that of Laban, who controls the sexual lives of his daughters and his son-in-law).

3. Boyarin, *Carnal Israel*, 148.
4. Luce Irigaray, *This Sex Which Is Not One*, trans. Catherine Porter (Ithaca, NY: Cornell University Press, 1985), ch. 6. We will not enter into a broad discussion of the cultural and theological place of crying in rabbinic literature. Studies dealing with the rabbinic as well as with the Greco-Roman worlds show that crying in early and late antiquity was a cultural practice adopted by both men and women, though in different modes and for different purposes. Noa Walden notes that rabbinic literature includes more than five hundred mentions of crying, many of them ascribed to men, among them R. Judah ha-Nasi, whose weeping is the topic of her Master's thesis. See Noa Walden, "Weeping in Rabbinic Literature: Cultural, Literary, and Rhetorical Aspects" (in Hebrew) (Master's thesis, Ben-Gurion University of the Negev, 2012). See also Shulamit Valler, *Sorrow and Distress in the Talmud*, trans. Sharon Blass (Boston: Academic Studies Press, 2011), 186–242.
5. In some manuscripts (MS Munich 95 and MS London Harl. 5508), the term "often" (*tadir*) replaces the term "much" (*yoter*), which appears in the printed version. The difference between these two terms is significant: Whereas "much" refers to excessive crying, "often" refers to persistent crying, whose power and threat derive from its ceaselessness.
6. Note that MS London does not mention the deaths of six more sons but only the deaths of the first son and the mother.
7. According to the printed version, it is Rav Huna who commands the woman's death, but according to two manuscripts (Munich 140 and Oxford), her death is a kind of suicide following from the death of all her sons: "She also made a shroud for herself and died."
8. Our brief discussion of the story is based, inter alia, on Noa Walden's address at the Yad Ben Zvi 2015 conference in Jerusalem, 5/7/2015. We thank her for her consent to make use of her lecture.
9. We cannot expand here on Rav Huna's talmudic biography and its connection to this story. Nevertheless, we will mention that, according to a story in BT Nazir, the sons of Rav Huna also died young after his

colleague, Rav Adda b. Ahavah, cursed Rav Huna's wife, whose name was Hoba: "Rav Huna said, 'One who rounds [the head of] a minor [that is, one who cuts his sons' hair without leaving ear locks] is liable.' Rav Adda b. Ahavah said to Rav Huna, 'And yours, who shaves them?' Said he, 'Hoba.' [He replied,] 'Hoba will bury her children.' During the whole of Rav Adda b. Ahavah's lifetime, none of Rav Huna's children survived." (BT Nazir 57b)

10. The rabbis' opposition to women showing excessive or exaggerated grief in scholarly or judicial ambits comes forth in the Babylonian Talmud in descriptions of screaming women in the study house or in judicial proceedings. The sages' reaction is described as "he paid no attention to her," conveying derision and unwillingness to conduct a dialogue with a woman who exceeds the bounds of a controlled discourse. See, for example, BT Shabbat 55a; Sukkah 31a; Ketubot 80b.
11. Evidence of the sages' recourse to verbal magic to determine people's destiny is widespread in rabbinic literature. Thus, for example, the various formulations of the idiom "the curse of a sage, even if uncalled for, is fulfilled" (see BT Sanhedrin 90b; Makkot 11a; Berakhot 56a) point to the sage's power to use his authority to decide people's fate. On this question, see Galit Hasan-Rokem, *Proverbs in Israeli Folk Narrative: A Structural Semantic Analysis* (Folklore Fellows Communications, 232) (Helsinki: Suomalainen Tiedeakatemia, Academia Scientiarum Fennica, 1982), 66; Haim Weiss, *All Dreams Follow the Mouth: A Reading in the Talmudic Dreams Tractate* (in Hebrew) (Or Yehuda: Kinneret, Zmora, Bitan/Dvir, 2011), 161–162.
12. A further expression, although from a slightly different perspective, of a woman's willingness to sacrifice her sons as part of a struggle appears in a story cited in Leviticus Rabba: A woman swears in vain on the life of her three sons (and consequently kills them) to save herself when she is accused of being a thief. For the story, see Leviticus Rabba 6:3. For an extensive discussion of this story, see Galit Hasan-Rokem, *Tales of the Neighborhood: Jewish Narrative Dialogues in Late Antiquity* (Berkeley: University of California Press, 2003), 14–27.
13. As Walden notes, this story is reminiscent of a more famous account of martyrdom: the story of the mother and her seven sons who were killed

by the emperor. There are several versions of this tale; the earliest seems to be the one that appears in 2 Maccabees, Ch. 7. There are additional versions in Lamentations Rabba 1 and in legends about the destruction of the Temple in the Babylonian Talmud, Gittin 56b. In this context, see Galit Hasan-Rokem, *Web of Life: Folklore and Midrash in Rabbinic Literature,* trans. Batya Stein (Stanford, CA: Stanford University Press, 2000), 114–125, and the relevant bibliography there. On the men's regimentation of women's mourning, particularly in contexts of lamentation and sorrow expressed through physical gestures, see Vered Madar, "Yemenite Women's Songs for the Parturient and Their Laments Over the Dead: Text, Body, and Voice" (in Hebrew) (PhD diss., Hebrew University of Jerusalem, 2011), especially 284–286.

14. The theological power of a woman's tears, and more precisely the tears of a wife whose husband has lied, is reflected in the words of Rav and R. Elazar: "Rav said: A man should always be careful not to hurt his wife because, since her tears are frequent, she is quickly hurt. R. Elazar said: Since the destruction of the Temple, the gates of prayer are locked . . . but although the gates of prayer are locked, the gates of tears are not" (BT Bava Meziah 59a). See also Charlotte Elisheva Fonrobert, "When the Rabbi Weeps: On Reading Gender in Talmudic Aggadah," *Nashim: A Journal of Jewish Women's Studies & Gender Issues* 4 (2001): 56–83.
15. For a parallel version of the Babylonian Talmud's story, see Lamentations Rabba 3. For studies on the story, see, for example Yona Fraenkel, *On Aggadah and Midrash* (in Hebrew) (Ramat-Gan: Yad la-Talmud, 1991), 241–242; Admiel Kosman, *Men's World: Reading Masculinity in Jewish Stories in a Spiritual Context,* trans. Edward Levin (Würzburg: Ergon, 2009), 67–71; Ronit Shoshany, "The Story of the Carpenter's Apprentice" (in Hebrew), *Sidra: A Journal for the Study of Rabbinic Literature* 21 (2006): 87-98; Shmuel Faust, *Agadata: Stories of Talmudic Drama* (in Hebrew) (Or Yehuda: Kinneret/Zmora Bitan/Dvir, 2011).
16. Julia Kristeva, "Women's Time," trans. Alice Jardine and Harry Blake, *Signs* 7, no. 1 (1981): 16.
17. See also Boyarin, *Carnal Israel,* 147–148.
18. We used the NRSV for translations of biblical texts, except for a few isolated instances where the RSV proved to be more accurate.

19. According to Fraenkel, this was a later addition meant to "emphasize that these are not a student and a rabbi at the *beth midrash*" (Fraenkel, *On Aggadah and Midrash*, 241). Note that, in the manuscripts known to us, all of which include the Aramaic expression, there is no evidence for Fraenkel's claim.
20. Each manuscript suggests a different version of the phrase "he stayed with her." The manuscripts' many versions of her stay in the apprentice's house attest to the tension surrounding the woman's character in the story and to the various ways to understand the nature of her stay and, consequently, her move from the rabbi to the apprentice. As Hasan-Rokem and Admiel Kosman point out, the fact that the woman has no voice of her own highlights her objectification by the two men and her function as a reward to the winner in the struggle. See Galit Hasan-Rokem, "The Three-Folded Cord: On Sexuality, Couplehood, and Womanhood in Rabbinic Literature" (in Hebrew), *Theory and Criticism* 7 (1995): 255–264; Kosman, *Men's World*, 67–71.

SECOND STORY

1. See Shira Stav, *Reconstructing Daddy: Fathers and Daughters in Modern Hebrew Poetry* (in Hebrew) (Or Yehuda: Dvir, 2014), 20, and references. On the daughters of Zelophehad, see Tal Ilan, "The Daughters of Zelophehad and Women's Inheritance: The Biblical Injunction and Its Outcome," in *A Feminist Companion to the Bible: Exodus to Deuteronomy* (second series), ed. Athalya Brenner (Sheffield: Sheffield Academic Press, 2000), 176–186.
2. Claude Lévi-Strauss, *The Elementary Structures of Kinship*, trans. James Harle Bell (Boston: Beacon Press, 1969), 115.
3. Lynda E. Boose, "The Father's House and the Daughter in It," in *Daughters and Fathers*, ed. Lynda E. Boose and Betty S. Flowers (Baltimore, MD: Johns Hopkins University Press, 1989), 19.
4. Hortense Spillers, "'The Permanent Obliquity of an In[pha]llibly Straight': In the Time of the Daughters and Fathers," in *Daughters and Fathers*, ed. Boose and Flowers, 157. See also Stav, *Reconstructing Daddy*, 20.

5. Freud's disciple Otto Rank, a psychoanalyst and scholar of myths, similarly argues that the drama of the father-daughter relationship is always presented from the father's perspective. See Otto Rank, *The Incest Theme in Literature and Legend: Fundamentals of a Psychology of Literary Creation*, trans. Gregory C. Richter (Baltimore, MD: Johns Hopkins University Press, 1992), 301.
6. Yona Fraenkel, *Studies on the Spiritual World of the Aggadic Story* (in Hebrew) (Tel Aviv: Hakibbutz Hameuchad, 1981), 103.
7. Daniel Boyarin, *Carnal Israel: Reading Sex in Talmudic Culture* (Berkeley: University of California Press, 1993), 149. Jeffrey Rubenstein ties together Fraenkel's and Boyarin's views. See Jeffrey L. Rubenstein, *The Culture of the Babylonian Talmud* (Baltimore, MD: Johns Hopkins University Press, 2003), 106.
8. According to Boyarin, "The fact that Judah's procession to his home is preceded by a pillar of fire, the very sign that led the Jews in the Wilderness and brought them to the Promised Land, is a strong indication that we are not to read the narrative as a conflict of values." Boyarin, *Carnal Israel*, 149.
9. The Ben Sira version is similar in structure and in the anxious attitude it conveys, but different in several details: "A daughter is a treasure that keeps her father wakeful, and worry over her drives away sleep: Lest in her youth she remain unmarried, or when she is married, lest she be childless; While unmarried, lest she be defiled, or in her husband's house, lest she prove unfaithful; Lest she become pregnant in her father's house, or be sterile in that of her husband" (*The Book of Ben Sira or Sirach* 42: 9–10, https://biblescripture.net/Sirach.html [accessed June 6, 2020]).
10. See Stav, *Reconstructing Daddy*, 21.
11. In MS Munich 95, there is no mention of a hole in the fence, and looking is an open and direct act.
12. The words "may they not transgress because of you" do not appear in MS Munich 140 and in MS Oxford.
13. This is the third in a sequence of four talmudic stories singling out R. Jose of Yokeret. In the second story, R. Jose of Yokeret is described as controlling the behavior of his son. Following what R. Jose considers

inappropriate conduct by his son—resorting to magic practices to force a fig tree to give fruit not in its time—R. Jose condemns him to death: "He said to his son, 'My son, you have troubled your Creator to cause the fig tree to bring forth its fruit before its time, may you be taken before your time'" (BT Ta`anit 24a). In this context, see Fraenkel, *Studies on the Spiritual World*, 36–40; Menachem Katz and Israel Rosensohn, "'Fig, Bring Forth Your Fruit': The Stories of R. Jose of Yokeret" (in Hebrew), *Derekh Aggadah* 3 (2000): 161–177; Admiel Kosman, *Men's World: Reading Masculinity in Jewish Stories in a Spiritual Context*, trans. Edward Levin (Würzburg: Ergon, 2009), 61–66; Shmuel Faust, "Criticism in Sages' Stories from the Babylonian Talmud" (PhD diss., Bar-Ilan University, 2010), 117–120; Tsafi Sebba-Elran, "R. Yossi of Yokeret and the Modern Jewish Anthologies" (in Hebrew), in *Folklore and Ideology: Studies Dedicated to Prof. Aliza Shenhar,* ed. Haya Bar-Itzhak (Haifa: Pardes, 2014), 133–163.

14. Faust, "Criticism," 118.
15. The importance of the father's and the law's control over the space surrounding the home is evident in the detailed laws in M. Bava Bathra concerning the building of fences and hedges between houses, especially on the question of how and under what limitations one is allowed to cut an opening that faces a neighbor's courtyard. See, for example, M. Bava Bathra 1:3, 7.
16. See Sebba-Elran, "R. Yossi of Yokeret," 135. Sebba-Elran mentions an identical linguistic formulation, "return to your dust," which R. Zera uses to kill the *golem* created by Rava. See BT Sanhedrin 65b.
17. Freud determines that scopophilia (the pleasure of watching others) is a significant element of sexuality, sustained as an independent impulse. Scopophilia is related to the possibility of watching the other as an object subjected to a curious and penetrating gaze and deriving erotic pleasure from it. See Sigmund Freud, *On Sexuality: Three Essays on the Theory of Sexuality*, trans. James Strachey (London: Penguin Books, 1991). Slavoj Žižek's insights on the voyeuristic act reverse the Freudian center of gravity: In contrast to the idea that looking at a woman causes sexual pleasure to the male voyeur, Žižek's claim is that the voyeur is the one who is reduced to the rank of an object in the power relationship established

through the gaze, since he is paralyzed from any possibility of action. See Slavoj Žižek, *Looking Awry: An Introduction to Jacques Lacan Through Popular Culture* (Cambridge, MA: MIT Press, 1993), 109–110. This idea deepens the possibility that the father imposes a death sentence on his daughter to compensate for the harm the pleasure of the gaze inflicted on his patriarchal power. In her brief analysis of the story, Esther Fisher emphasizes the unified male gaze of the voyeur and of the father. Moreover, she adds other potential voyeurs, such as the editor and the reader, who also look at the beautiful daughter through the gaze of the father and the voyeur. See Esther Fisher, "'His *Yetzer* Is External, Her *Yetzer* Is Internal': Gendered Aspects of Sexual Desire in Rabbinic Literature" (in Hebrew) (PhD diss., Bar-Ilan University, 2014), 67. See also Rachael Neis, *The Sense of Sight in Rabbinic Culture: Jewish Ways of Seeing in Late Antiquity* (Cambridge University Press, 2013), 113-169.

18. See Jane Gallop, *The Daughter's Seduction: Feminism and Psychoanalysis* (Ithaca, NY: Cornell University Press, 1982), 77.

19. Another talmudic expression of the father's desire for control or for presence in the sexual acts of his daughters is Rav Hisda's advice to his daughters, touching on their behavior with their husbands at all times of day and particularly during the sexual act: "Rav Hisda advised his daughters, 'Act modestly before your men [your husbands]—do not eat bread before your men, do not eat greens at night, do not eat dates at night nor drink beer at night, and do not relieve yourselves where your men relieve themselves, and when someone calls at the door, do not say 'who is it' in the masculine form but in the feminine one.' He took a pearl in one hand and a seed grain in the other; he showed them the pearl but did not show them the seed grain until they were aching, and then he showed it to them" (BT Shabbat 140b). Rav Hisda's advice to his daughters attests to encroachment into the most intimate areas of the body and the conjugal relationship—sex, eating, and defecation—clearly and distinctly separating the daughters from their husbands. Furthermore, Rav Hisda creates here a situation of gender reversal, where he becomes the seductive female while his daughters represent the male desire. This gender reversal can also be tied to his preference for daughters over sons: "Rav Hisda said, 'To me, daughters are dearer than sons'" (Bava Bathra 141a).

20. Interesting support for such a reading emerges from two manuscript versions of the story (Vatican 113 and Vatican 487.11), which read "lower my bed" rather than "lower his bed," meaning that R. Yannai asks for his bed to be turned over in a sign of mourning for R. Judah's death and, consequently, the elimination of the sexual option between them. The source of the custom to turn over one's bed in a sign of mourning, which was widespread in the Land of Israel and in Babylonia, appears in the Babylonian Talmud in Mo'ed Katan 16a. For a discussion of the laws about lowering the bed, see Yitzhak Zimmer, "Lowering the Bed in Mourning" (in Hebrew), *Sinai* 115 (1995): 228–252; Nissan Rubin, *The End of Life: Rites of Burial and Mourning in the Talmud and Midrash* (in Hebrew) (Tel Aviv: Hakibbutz Hameuchad, 1997), 172–173.
21. On the difference between the Palestinian and the Babylonian versions, see Tal Ilan, *Mine and Yours Are Hers: Retrieving Women's History from Rabbinic Literature* (Leiden: Brill, 1997), 209; Yeshayahu Ben-Pazzi, "The Biblical and Midrashic Context as a Tool in the Understanding of Rabbinic Aggadot" (in Hebrew), *Hemdat* 6 (2009): 47–71.
22. René Girard, *Deceit, Desire, and the Novel: Self and Other in Literary Structure*, trans. Yvonne Freccero (Baltimore, MD: Johns Hopkins University Press, 1972).
23. Ibid., 362.
24. Eve Kosofsky Sedgwick, *Between Men: English Literature and Male Homosocial Desire* (New York: Columbia University Press, 1985).

THIRD STORY

1. Gayle Rubin, "The Traffic in Women: Notes on the 'Political Economy' of Sex," in *Toward an Anthropology of Women*, ed. Rayna Reiter (New York: Monthly Review Press, 1975), 157–210. Rubin criticizes the approach of Lévi-Strauss—which seeks "to celebrate" the movement of women between men as an enormous social achievement and a foundation of heterosexual romanticism—and suggests thinking about exogamy as a mechanism for preserving patriarchal power and control over women.
2. Heidi Hartmann, "The Unhappy Marriage of Marxism and Feminism: Towards a More Progressive Union," in *Feminist Theory Reader: Local*

and Global Perspectives, ed. Carole McCann and Seung-Kyung Kim (New York: Routledge, 2017), 219.

3. He says: "This story is a Babylonian fiction. There is not one hint of this event in Palestinian sources. . . . The story's focus is a quintessential concern of Babylonian sages: lineage (*yihus*)." Jeffrey L. Rubenstein, *The Culture of the Babylonian Talmud* (Baltimore, MD: Johns Hopkins University Press, 2003), 81. See also Dina Stein, "Collapsing Structures: Discourse and the Destruction of the Temple in the Babylonian Talmud," *Jewish Quarterly Review* 98, no. 1 (2008): 15.
4. "Sons were born to David at Hebron: his firstborn was Amnon, of Ahinoam of Jezreel; his second, Chileab, of Abigail the widow of Nabal of Carmel; the third, Absalom son of Maacah, daughter of King Talmai of Geshur; the fourth, Adonijah son of Haggith; the fifth, Shephatiah son of Abital; and the sixth, Ithream, of David's wife Eglah. These were born to David in Hebron" (2 Sam. 3:2–5). See Aharon Oppenheimer, *Rabbi Judah ha-Nasi* (in Hebrew) (Jerusalem: Zalman Shazar Center for Jewish History, 2007), 24, and the discussion there on the various options of lineage.
5. Shimei, David's brother, is mentioned several times in Scripture. See, for example, 2 Sam. 13:33, 1 Chr. 2:13. The purported lineage flaw may derive from Rabbi's wish to detach David from his dynasty of origin. Both David and his brother Shimei are the sons of Jesse and descendants from the mythological family that began with the marriage of Boaz and Ruth, the Moabite. In this context, Ruth Kara-Ivanov Kaniel points to the dubious origins of the Davidic biblical dynasty. See Ruth Kara-Ivanov Kaniel, *Holiness and Transgression: Mothers of the Messiah in the Jewish Myth*, trans. Eugene D. Matanky with Ruth Kara-Ivanov Kaniel (Boston: Academic Studies Press, 2017).
6. For a discussion of all the sources dealing with Rabbi's ancestry, including those where he confronts R. Hiyah and his descendants, see Ofra Meir, *R. Judah the Patriarch: Palestinian and Babylonian Portrait of a Leader* (in Hebrew) (Tel Aviv: Hakibbutz Hameuchad, 1999), 27–33.
7. For a parallel version, see Genesis Rabba 33. For a partial parallel version, which preserves the angry dialogue between Rabbi and R. Hiyah at the end of the story, see BT Mo'ed Katan 16a–b. A further reflection

of the tension between Rabbi and R. Hiyah over the question of Rabbi's standing vis-à-vis the exilarch emerges in a discussion between them in BT Horayot 11b.

8. The Palestinian source claims that Rabbi's lineage was actually flawed and female, in contrast to the Babylonian source, which suggests an unblemished lineage. In this context, Meir claims: "It appears that, in Palestine, Rabbi was seen as a descendant of Hillel, and the Davidic lineage was known but was not perceived as certain and definitive." See Meir, *R. Judah the Patriarch*, 29. On this issue, see also Rubenstein, *The Culture of the Babylonian Talmud*, 82, who claims that the gap between the Palestinian and the Babylonian ancestry exposes the importance that Babylonian Jews ascribed to this question.
9. See Oppenheimer, *Rabbi Judah ha-Nasi*, 145.
10. In her discussion of this story, Meir deals only with the first part, without addressing at all the second, which includes the confrontation between R. Hiyah and R. Judah ha-Nasi. See Meir, *R. Judah ha-Nasi*, 28–29.
11. For another source describing a physical response by R. Judah ha-Nasi to a status threat, see PT Shabbat 10:5.
12. In the parallel version in Genesis Rabbah mentioned earlier, the end of the story is not confined to a somewhat vague claim—"[he] understood that he was angry with him." Instead, it describes R. Hiyah as one who "rebuked" himself and refrained from approaching Rabbi for thirty days.
13. A further interesting expression of Rabbi's stance, whereby daughters would not be part of the family's dynastic continuity and would not return to it, appears in Genesis Rabbah. The midrash describes another status dispute between R. Hiyah and R. Judah ha-Nasi, who suggest different and largely contradictory responses to the birth of Rabbi's granddaughter: "The wife of R. Shimon, the son of Rabbi, gave birth to a daughter. R. Hiyah the Elder saw him [Shimon] and said to him: 'The Holy One, blessed be He, has begun to bless you.' Said he, 'Whence do you know that?' Said he, 'Because it is written, "When people began to multiply" [on the face of the ground, and daughters were born to them]' (Gen. 6:1). He [R. Shimon] went to his father, who asked him, 'Did the Babylonian [intending R. Hiyah, who is of

Babylonian origin] congratulate you?' Said he, 'Yes, and this is what he said to me.' Said he [Rabbi], 'Although we need both wine and vinegar, we need more wine than vinegar. We need both wheat and barley, yet we need more wheat than barley. *After a man has married off his daughter and spent his money, he says to her, "you have nowhere to come back to"*'" (Genesis Rabbah 26, our emphasis). See also Meir, *R. Judah ha-Nasi*, 51.

14. On this issue, see David Zimmerman, *Eight Love Stories from Talmud and Midrash* (in Hebrew) (Tel Aviv: Sifriat Poalim, 1981), 32.
15. Boyarin, *Carnal Israel*, 138–142.
16. *Mekhilta de-Rabbi Ishmael*, trans. Jacob Z. Lauterbach, vol. 1 (Philadelphia: Jewish Publication Society, 2004), Tractate *Shirata*, ch. X, 217. See also *The Fathers According to Rabbi Nathan*, trans. Anthony J. Saldarini (Leiden: Brill, 1975) version B, ch. 43.
17. See Stein, "Collapsing Structures," 15–16.
18. Meir also pointed out the prominent role of the father in the story and viewed it as a sign of his being "a caring, involved father, sensitive and yet extremely dominant" (Meir, *R. Judah ha-Nasi*, 65).
19. R. Judah ha-Nasi's suggestion raises the question of polygamy at the time of the *tannaim* and the *amoraim*. This question, which we are not trying to decide here, is in dispute among scholars. Gedalyahu Alon conveys a widespread view among scholars: "Until such time as the opposite is proven, we must say that Jews actually refrained, except in special cases, from marrying two or more women" (Gedalyahu Alon, "The Sociological Method in the Study of Halakhah," in *Studies in Jewish History in the Times of the Second Temple, the Mishnah and the Talmud* [in Hebrew] [Tel Aviv: Hakibbutz Hameuchad, 1978] 188, n. 12). For a different view, see Adiel Schremer, *Male and Female He Created Them: Jewish Marriage in the Late Second Temple, Mishnah, and Talmud Periods* (in Hebrew) (Jerusalem: Zalman Shazar Center for Jewish History, 2003), 193–218.
20. This was not the only time that the marriages of R. Judah ha-Nasi's children were associated with licentiousness. The following story appears in BT Bava Meziah (85a): "Rabbi happened to visit the town of R. Tarfon and said to them: 'Does he have a son, that righteous man who used to

swear by the life of his children?' They replied: 'He has no son, he has a daughter's son, and every whore hired for two hires him for eight.' They brought him [the grandson] before him and he said to him: 'If you mend your ways, I will give you my daughter.' He mended his ways. Some say he married her [Rabbi's daughter] and divorced her, some say he did not marry her at all so it would not be said he mended his ways for that." On this issue, see Oppenheimer, *Rabbi Judah ha-Nasi*, 24, who shows how R. Judah ha-Nasi's concern with lineage purity, as it is presented in Babylonian sources, led him to marry off his daughter to R. Tarfon's grandson despite his dubious past, given his grandfather's lineage.

21. On the archetypes of Eve and Lilith, see Nitza Abarbanell, *Eve and Lilith* (in Hebrew) (Ramat-Gan: Bar-Ilan University Press, 1994); Ohad Ezrahi and Mordechai Gafni, *Who's Afraid of Lilith: Re-reading the Kabbalah of the Feminine Shadow* (in Hebrew) (Ben-Shemen: Modan, 2005). Evidence of the tension between these two polarized female representations—the domestic, childbearing, asexual woman versus the boundless sexuality of the whore—appears in a story that fuses the two representations. In Sifrei Numbers there is a story about a student of R. Hiyah who was fond of prostitutes: "Once there was a man who carefully observed the commandment of *tsitsit* [ritual fringes]. He heard that there was a whore in a city by the sea whose fee was four hundred gold coins. He sent her four hundred gold coins, and she set a time for him. When his appointed time came, he went and waited at her doorstep. Her maid went in and told her that the man she had set time for was sitting at her doorstep. Said she, 'Let him come in.' When he came in, she prepared for him seven beds of silver and one of gold. She was at the top one, and between them were steps of silver and the top one of gold. As they came to perform the act, his four fringes seemed to him as four witnesses that struck him across his face. He then slipped and he sat on the ground, and she too slipped and sat on the ground. Said she, 'by the Love of Rome, I will not leave you until you tell me—what is the flaw you saw on me?' Said he, 'By the Temple, I saw no flaw in you and none is as beautiful as you in the entire world, but the Lord our God has commanded us a minor commandment and wrote in it, "I am the Lord your God" "I am the Lord your God" twice—I am the Lord your God and

will in the future reward you, I am the Lord your God and will in the future exact payment.' Said she, 'By the Temple, I will not leave you until you write down for me your name, the name of your city, and the name of the school where you study Torah.' And he wrote for her his name, and the name of his city and the name of his rabbi and the name of the school where he studied Torah. She stood up and divided her wealth—one third for the government, one third for the poor, and one third she took with her. She then went to R. Hiyah's study house and said to him, 'Rabbi, make me a Jew.' Said he, 'Have you set your eyes on one of the students?' She took out the script she had. Said he to him, 'Go, and enjoy your possession. The very bed clothes she had spread for you unlawfully she will now spread out for you lawfully. This is the reward [of the commandment] in this world and as for its reward in the world to come, I do not know how much it is'" (Sifre Numbers, 115). This story, of which there is a parallel version in BT Menahot 44a, reflects a powerful male romantic fantasy that fundamentally fuses the two contradictory female representations of the saint and the whore into one single figure who is simultaneously the domestic and nondomestic woman—a fertile woman who also knows sexual desire. Here, too, as in the wedding story of Rabbi's son, we find prominent similarities with the biblical story of Tamar and Judah (as will be discussed shortly)—both because of the woman's sophistication and manipulation in asking for signs that will eventually serve as proof of previous acquaintance, and because of the fusion of the saint's and the whore's features in one single figure. For a broad discussion of the Sifrei Numbers story, see Mira Balberg, "Between Heterotopias and Utopias: Two Rabbinic Stories about Journeys to Prostitutes" (in Hebrew), *Jerusalem Studies in Hebrew Literature* 22 (2008): 191–213; Michal Bar-Asher Siegal, *Early Christian Monastic Literature and the Babylonian Talmud* (New York: Cambridge University Press, 2013), and the sources they note.

22. See Sigmund Freud, *On Sexuality: Three Essays on the Theory of Sexuality*, trans. James Strachey (London: Penguin Books, 1991), in the article, "A Special Type of Choice of Object Made by Men" (1910).
23. Kara-Ivanov Kaniel's book deals at length with "questionable copulation, embodying the paradoxical connection between transgression,

messianism, and redemption" in the Davidic dynasty. See her *Holiness and Transgression*, 1.

FOURTH STORY

1. See Shulamit Valler, *Women and Womanhood in the Talmud*, trans. Betty Sigler Rozen (Providence, RI: Brown University, 1999), 66–67.
2. Nissan Rubin, *The End of Life: Rites of Burial and Mourning in the Talmud and Midrash* (in Hebrew) (Tel Aviv: Hakibbutz Hameuchad, 1997), 238.
3. Thus, for example, the narrative tradition in Leviticus Rabba (20:3), about a dignitary who celebrated his son's wedding, describes a situation where the groom was left unprotected during the festivities and this led to his death. A similar story is also told about R. Akiva's daughter; see Galit Hasan-Rokem, "The Snake at the Wedding: Semiotic Reconsideration of the Comparative Method of Folk Narrative Research" (in Hebrew), *Criticism and Interpretation: Journal for Literature, Linguistics, History and Aesthetics* 30 (1994): 26–40. Ben Hakhinai's refusal to remain with his friend on the days of the banquet is the basis and starting point of the entire story. For a sociological reading of the ancient Jewish wedding ceremony that emphasizes its liminal aspects, see Nissan Rubin, *The Joy of Life: Rites of Betrothal and Marriage in the Talmud and Midrash* (in Hebrew) (Tel Aviv: Hakibbutz Hameuchad, 2004), 262–268.
4. The strategy of Ben Hakhinai, who tracks his daughter so that she will lead him to his home, recalls that of the wise son in the first of the riddle stories in Lamentations Rabba, which Galit Hasan-Rokem has discussed at length. According to the story, a Jerusalem man entrusted his belongings to his Athenian host, which were to be given to his son under certain conditions: "Should my son come to you and desire these belongings, don't give them to him unless he does three wise acts." The son's first wise act is to discover by himself where the host lives: "They [the Athenians] had [an agreement] that none of them would point the way to another person's house for a traveler. The son heard [of his father's death] and went there, knowing the name of the

man. He came and sat at the city gate, saw a man carrying a load of wood, and said, 'Are you selling that wood?' He said: 'Yes.' He says: 'Take payment and go to unload it [at so-and so's house].' He followed him until they arrived at the man's house. He [the woodcarrier] began calling for him. [The master of the house] looked through the window and asked: 'What do you want?' Said he: 'Come out and take the wood.' He said to him: 'Did I tell you to bring it to me?' He said: 'It's not yours, but belongs to the one sitting behind it.' He came down to ask who he was and said: 'Who are you?' He said to him: 'I am the son of the man from Jerusalem who died at your house.'" Lamentations Rabba (Buber) 1, cited in Galit Hasan-Rokem, *Web of Life: Folklore and Midrash in Rabbinic Literature*, trans. Batya Stein (Stanford, CA: Stanford University Press, 2000), 46–47. For a discussion of the story, see ibid., 52–57. Dina Stein, who also deals with the association between the story of Odysseus and the present story, emphasizes that Odysseus came in disguise so that he would not be recognized. By contrast, Ben Hakhinai does not need to do that, since his absence is his disguise. See Dina Stein, "Identity, Absence, and Return: Reading Two Rabbinic Stories" (in Hebrew), in *Childhood Memory and Forgetfulness: Revisiting Odysseus' Scar*, ed. Vered Lev Kenaan and Noga Weiss (Haifa: Haifa University Press, 2018).

5. The sages' power to revive the dead is rarely noted but appears in other places in rabbinic literature. One example is the story of Rabba and R. Zera, when Rabba, drunk after a Purim feast, murders R. Zera and the next morning, after sobering up, revives him (BT Megilah 7b); another is the story about the encounter of Rabbi and Antoninus, when R. Hanina b. Hama brings a dead guard back to life (BT Avodah Zarah 10b).
6. Robert Alter, *The Art of Biblical Narrative* (New York: Basic Books, 1981), 47–62.
7. On this issue, see ibid., 53: "this is in fact the only instance where a surrogate rather than the man himself meets the girl at the well. That substitution nicely accords with the entire career of Isaac, for he is manifestly the most passive of the patriarchs. We have already seen him as a bound victim for whose life a ram is substituted; later, as a father, he will prefer the son who can go out to the field and bring him back

provender, and his one extended scene will be lying in bed, weak and blind, while others act on him."

8. In this context, note also Dina Stein's claim: "The father found himself in a kind of betrothal scene" (Dina Stein, "Identity, Absence, and Return: Reading Two Rabbinic Stories" [in Hebrew], in *Childhood Memory and Forgetfulness: Revisiting Odysseus' Scar*, ed. Vered Lev Kenaan and Noga Weiss [Haifa: Haifa University Press, 2018], 189–201.). A similar course is evident in the story about Lot's daughters, where the mother's sexual decline is represented by her transformation into a pillar of salt, and her young daughters take her place as the father's erotic partners and as mothers of his children (Genesis 19).
9. This version appears in the Theodor-Albeck of Genesis Rabba. For another parallel version, see Leviticus Rabba 25:8. The significant difference suggested in Leviticus Rabba is that Ben Hakhinai first went to his house, but found that his family had moved. He went to look for them, and when he saw his daughter drawing water, he followed her. For an analysis of the Leviticus Rabba version, see Jeffrey L. Rubenstein, *The Culture of the Babylonian Talmud* (Baltimore, MD: Johns Hopkins University Press, 2003), 116–118.
10. According to Tal Ilan, not only did the Palestinian tradition precede the Babylonian one but the Babylonian tradition knew the earlier one and in a way reacted to it or completed it: "It is obvious that the *Babylonian Talmud* was familiar with this story. At some points it supplements it, at others it alters it for its own purpose" (Tal Ilan, *Mine and Yours Are Hers: Retrieving Women's History from Rabbinic Literature* [Leiden: Brill, 1997], 211). Daniel Boyarin also views the Babylonian version as a later version of the Palestinian one, and holds that the Babylonian version aims to soften or lighten the open critique that emerges from the Palestinian version: "The Babylonian version is a revision of the story, which is explicitly designed to provide a utopian solution to the enormous moral and halakhic contradictions involved in the practice of husbands being away from their wives to study Torah for years on end" (Daniel Boyarin, *Carnal Israel: Reading Sex in Talmudic Culture* [Berkeley: University of California Press, 1993], 158). Shulamit Valler also holds that the Babylonian version is a revised Palestinian

version, adapted to the contents of the narrative series in the Babylonian Talmud. See Valler, *Women and Womanhood*, 67.

11. The presentation of R. Shimon b. Yohai as constantly keeping in touch with his home and being interested in what happens with his family contradicts what is known to us from narrative traditions, both Palestinian and Babylonian, about his hiding in a cave for many years. For a discussion of these narrative traditions and their family and conjugal implications, see Haim Weiss, "Worthless Son of Worthy Father? Political Struggles, Torah Study, and Identity in the Family of R. Shimon Bar Yohai" (in Hebrew). In *Peace and War in Jewish Culture*, ed. Avriel Bar-Levav, 67–83 (Jerusalem: Zalman Shazar Center for Jewish History, 2006).
12. We thank Itamar Luria for this comment.
13. Judith R. Baskin, *Midrashic Women: Formations of the Feminine in Rabbinic Literature* (Hanover, NH: Brandeis University Press, 2002), 104.
14. Euripides, *Alcestis*, trans. David Kovacs (Cambridge, MA: Harvard University Press, 1994), lines 282–283.
15. For a summary of the plot and its various sources in Greek literature, see Aharon Shabtai, introduction to the Hebrew translation of *Alcestis* by Euripides (Jerusalem: Schocken, 1986), 12–13.
16. Ibid., 9.
17. Baskin, *Midrashic Women*, 104, and especially note 39.

THE FIFTH STORY

1. Yona Fraenkel, *Studies on the Spiritual World of the Aggadic Story* (in Hebrew) (Tel Aviv: Hakibbutz Hameuchad, 1981), 99–100.
2. Ibid., 109–111.
3. Daniel Boyarin, *Carnal Israel: Reading Sex in Talmudic Culture* (Berkeley: University of California Press, 1993), 198–220.
4. See also Haim Weiss, "Worthless Son of Worthy Father? Political Struggles, Torah Study, and Identity in the Family of R. Simon Bar Yohai" (in Hebrew), in *Peace and War in Jewish Culture,* ed. Avriel Bar-Levav (Jerusalem: Zalman Shazar Center for Jewish History, 2006), 67–83.
5. Dina Stein, *Maxims, Magic, Myth: A Folkloristic Perspective of Pirkei deRabbi Eliezer* (in Hebrew) (Jerusalem: Magnes Press, 2004), 116–158.
6. Fraenkel, *Studies*, 110.

7. Sigmund Freud, *Moses and Monotheism*, trans. Katherine Jones (London: Hogarth Press/ Institute of Psychoanalysis, 1939), 180.
8. David Lee Miller, "The Body of Fatherhood," *ANQ: A Quarterly Journal of Short Articles, Notes and Reviews* 15 (2002): 3–16.
9. Nancy Chodorow, *The Reproduction of Mothering: Psychoanalysis and the Sociology of Gender* (Berkeley: University of California Press, 1979), 80.
10. Jacques Lacan, *Écrits: A Selection*, trans. Alan Sheridan (London: Tavistock, 1977), 67. As Jacqueline Rose shows, this is a "metaphor" for three main reasons: first, because it accepts the Oedipal proscription whereby the father's law replaces the mother's desire; second, due to the status of fatherhood itself which, as noted, is only inferred and derived; and third, because the "father" category cannot be reduced to the specific existence of any concrete father. See Jacqueline Rose, "Introduction—II," to Jacques Lacan, *Feminine Sexuality: Jacques Lacan and the École Freudienne*, trans. Jacqueline Rose (New York: Pantheon Books, 1985), 39.
11. On the use of biblical verses as proverbs, see Galit Hasan-Rokem, "The Biblical Verse as Proverb and as Quote" (in Hebrew), *Jerusalem Studies in Hebrew Literature* 1 (1981): 155–166.

THE SIXTH STORY

1. BT Nedarim 50a. Shamma Friedman, in an extensive comparative discussion of the two versions, claims that the Ketubot story is the original and the Nedarim text expands on it. See Shamma Friedman, "A Good Story Deserves Retelling: The Unfolding of the Akiva Legend," in *Creation and Composition: The Contribution of the Bavli Redactors (Stammaim) to the Aggadah*, ed. Jeffrey L. Rubenstein (Tübingen: Mohr-Siebeck, 2005), 79. See also Tal Ilan, *Mine and Yours Are Hers: Retrieving Women's History from Rabbinic Literature* (Leiden: Brill, 1997), 37–38; Itay Marienberg-Milikowsky, "'Beyond the Matter': Stories and Their Contexts in the Babylonian Talmud—Repeated Stories as a Test Case" (in Hebrew) (PhD diss., Ben-Gurion University of the Negev, 2015), 111–113. For a different version of the story about R. Akiva's beginnings, which describes him and his son going to study Torah together, see *The Fathers According to Rabbi Nathan*, trans. Judah

Goldin (New Haven, CT: Yale University Press, 1955), version A, ch. 6. In this context, see Jacob Elbaum, "Models of Storytelling and Speech in Stories about the Sages" (in Hebrew), *Proceedings of the Seventh World Congress of Jewish Studies* 7 (1977): 71–77. On the historical foundations of the story, see Shmuel Safrai, *R. Akiva ben Yosef: His Life and Teachings* (in Hebrew) (Jerusalem: Bialik Institute, 1978), 9–16.

2. Testimonies on the basic story about R. Akiva's wife's suffering during his years of study and the wealth that accompanied R. Akiva's rise to greatness are also found in Palestinian literary sources. See PT Sotah 9:15; PT Shabbat 6:1.
3. Yona Fraenkel, *Studies on the Spiritual World of the Aggadic Story* (in Hebrew) (Tel Aviv: Hakibbutz Hameuchad, 1981), 115.
4. Shulamit Valler, *Women and Womanhood in the Talmud*, trans. Betty Sigler Rozen (Providence, RI: Brown University, 1999), 71. See also Oded Israeli, "*Kiddushin*, Marriage, and Torah Study in the Stories of R. Akiva and the Daughter of Kalba Savu`a" (in Hebrew), *Assufot: Journal on Aggadah and Midrash* 1 (2010–2011): 94–104, who suggests a similar reading.
5. Valler, *Women and Womanhood*, 53. In this context, see also the view of Moshe Lavee: "Rachel is presented here as a daughter who rebels against her father. Strongminded, she chooses a man she wants and is eventually proven right, when he is revealed as a great Torah sage. By then the father, too, thanks his daughter and gives her half of his wealth. The story enables a view of Rachel as an exemplary model not only in her relationship with her husband but also in her steadfast stand against her father" (Moshe Lavee, "Acceptance of Other and Otherness: Processes of Emphasis and Ambiguity in Rabbinic Narratives." [in Hebrew], 37 [2001]: 75–114. Dror Eydar presents a similar approach and spices it up with a national flavor: "Because that indeed is the intent of the entire story: to position a woman's devotion to her husband against all odds, and its decisive importance for the Torah's survival . . . R. Akiva's wife joins here a whole tradition of biblical and post-biblical female figures standing at historical crossroads crucial to the development of the Jewish people, whose ways helped to direct their husbands to the spiritual, cultural, and political decisions that were warranted. And so in our story,

when the editor adopted the suitable perspective of evaluating the vital significance of R. Akiva for the preservation of halakhic and Torah tradition and the fostering of the people's national yearnings that, without the actions of his wife, would have been denied to the Jewish people" (Dror Eydar, "The Art of the Jewish-Persian Tale in the Middle Ages: A Study of the Story of R. Akiva and His Wife in Fourteenth- and Sixteenth-Century Manuscripts" [in Hebrew], *Jewish Studies Internet Journal* 9 [2010]: 103). Richard Kalmin views the marriage presented here as an instance of the Palestinian sages' inclination to encourage marriages between scholars and daughters of rich families. See Richard Kalmin, *The Sage in Jewish Society of Late Antiquity* (London: Routledge, 1999), 31.

6. Ilan, *Mine and Yours Are Hers*, 213. In a later article Ilan claims that this is a perfect story: "R. Akiva behaved fittingly toward his wife, and she also behaved in exemplary fashion toward him, and, therefore, no misfortune befell them." See Tal Ilan, "'Jerusalem of Gold' and the Historical Kernel in the Stories of R. Akiva's Wife" (in Hebrew), in *A Woman in Jerusalem: Gender, Society, and Religion*, ed. Tova Cohen and Joshua Schwartz (Ramat-Gan: Bar Ilan University Press, 2002), 33–46. For further discussion of the narrative dialogue between the story of R. Akiva and his wife and the story of Odysseus and Penelope, see Molly Myerowitz Levine, "Women Who Wait: Akiva's Rahel and Odysseus' Penelope," in *Hellenic and Jewish Arts: Interaction, Tradition and Renewal*, ed. Asher Ovadiah (Tel Aviv: Ramot, 1998).
7. Daniel Boyarin, *Carnal Israel: Reading Sex in Talmudic Culture* (Berkeley: University of California Press, 1993), 154. For assertions in this spirit, see Michael L. Satlow, *Jewish Marriage in Antiquity* (Princeton, NJ: Princeton University Press, 2001); Adiel Schremer, *Male and Female He Created Them: Jewish Marriage in the Late Second Temple, Mishnah, and Talmud Periods* (in Hebrew) (Jerusalem: Zalman Shazar Center for Jewish History, 2003), 68. See also Leila Leah Bronner, *From Eve to Esther: Rabbinic Reconstructions of Biblical Women* (Louisville, KY: Westminster John Knox Press, 1994), 9; Jeffrey L. Rubenstein, *Rabbinic Stories* (New York: Paulist Press, 2002), 141.
8. Boyarin, *Carnal Israel*, 142.

9. Ibid., 153. For references to the name of R. Akiva's wife, see the account in *Avot de-Rabbi Nathan* (Version A), where the name Rachel appears: "In the future, at Judgment, Rabbi Akiva will put all the poor in a guilty light. For if they are asked, 'Why did you not study Torah?' and they say, 'Because we were poor,' they shall be told: 'Indeed, was not Rabbi Akiva even poorer and in more wretched circumstances!' And if they say, 'Because of our children,' they shall be asked, 'And did not Rabbi Akiva have sons and daughters?' But they are told: 'Because Rachel, his wife, had merit.'" *The Fathers According to Rabbi Nathan*, trans. Goldin, ch. 6, 42. In his discussion of this story, Boyarin uses the name "Rachel" and even sees it as a key to the hermeneutical move he proposes. By contrast, Ilan and Friedman claim that we have no historical evidence that Rachel was her name. See Ilan, *Mine and Yours Are Hers*, 291; Friedman, "A Good Story," 82–83. See also Boyarin, *Carnal Israel*, 151–152, and n. 31; Avigdor Shinan, "The Three Wives of R. Akiva" (in Hebrew), *Masekhet* 2 (2004): 20; Susan Marks, "Follow That Crown: Or, Rhetoric, Rabbis, and Women Patrons," *Journal of Feminist Studies in Religion* 24 (2008): 77, n. 1.
10. Along this continuum, another interpretation of the share of R. Akiva's wife in encouraging her husband to leave for prolonged studies is also possible. Since the story does not disclose the participants' feelings, and we deduce them from their actions, there is also room for the hypothesis that her reaction on hearing of R. Akiva's return after twelve years—"Were I the one he listens to, he would go away to study for another twelve years"—could also indirectly convey her contentment with the freedom and independence she had gained in the long years without him and her wish to extend this time as much as possible.
11. Supporting evidence for R. Akiva's recognition of the enormous costs incurred by his wife is found in another source describing his decision, after he became wealthy, to give his wife expensive and lavish gifts that were the object of public criticism: "It is said: Before he departed from the world he owned tables of silver and gold, and mounted his couch on ladders of gold. His wife used to go about in golden sandals and in a golden tiara. 'Master,' his disciples said to him, 'thou hast put us to shame by what thou hast done for her.' He said to them: 'Many were the

trials she endured for my sake, that I might study Torah'" (*The Fathers According to Rabbi Nathan*, trans. Goldin, ch. 6, 42). On the significance of R. Akiva's wife's wealth, and particularly the prominent representation of this wealth in the "Jerusalem of gold" diadem, see Ilan, "Jerusalem of Gold."

12. Eve Kosofsky Sedgwick, *Between Men: English Literature and Male Homosocial Desire* (New York: Columbia University Press, 1985), and see the discussion at the end of "The Third Story," in this volume.
13. What emerges from this version of the story is that R. Akiva was betrothed to Ben Kalba Savu'a's daughter before leaving to study at the *beth midrash* but did not marry her, so that all these years she was actually forbidden to everybody else and could not marry. Her liminal state is highlighted against the background of the story's parallel version in BT Nedarim, which describes the betrothal and then the marriage, including a description of their conjugal relationship before his leaving home to study Torah.
14. The proverb "Ewe follows ewe" features only in the printed version and in MS Vatican 113. The other versions include the opening "and on this people say," pointing to the inclusion of a proverb, but the proverb they allude to is what in the printed version appears as the proverb's interpretation, "like mother, like daughter." Still, all the versions that have reached us indicate there is a proverb, and they differ regarding what the proverb is and what its interpretation is. According to Friedman, the phrase "Ewe follows ewe" is a later addition. See Friedman, "A Good Story," 81–82. Another rabbinic analogy tying the mother's actions to those of the daughter is found in their interpretation of the affair of Dina. In Genesis Rabba, the verse in Gen. 34:1, "Dina, the daughter of Leah . . . went out" is interpreted as evidence of "like mother, like daughter," except that the context there is explicitly negative and misogynous and attempts to present Leah, and in her wake Dina, as slutty and seductive. See Genesis Rabba 80.
15. Ben Kalba Savu'a's vow regarding his daughter is reminiscent of the story about R. Eliezer b. Hyrkanus's father, who vowed against him because he chose to study Torah with R. Yohanan b. Zakkai. In this case, too, the story ends with release from the vow and the award of the inheritance to

the son who had been banned and is now chosen. Dina Stein, who discusses at length several versions of the story about R. Eliezer b. Hyrkanus, views the revocation of the ban as attesting to "the vast power of the *beth midrash* as an institution conferring stability and a cultural identity by contrast with the institution of the family, which plays no role in attending to these needs." These statements seem to apply just as well to the story of R. Akiva discussed here. See Dina Stein, *Maxims, Magic, Myth: A Folkloristic Perspective of Pirkei deRabbi Eliezer* (in Hebrew) (Jerusalem: Magnes Press, 2004), 137–138.

16. Nancy Chodorow, *The Reproduction of Mothering: Psychoanalysis and the Sociology of Gender* (Berkeley: University of California Press, 1979).
17. *The Midrash on Psalms*, trans. William G. Braude, vol. 1 (New Haven, CT: Yale University Press, 1959), Psalm 59, 510.
18. For further discussion, see Admiel Kosman, *Women's Tractate: Wisdom, Love, Faithfulness, Passion, Beauty, Sex, Holiness* (in Hebrew) (Jerusalem: Keter, 2007).
19. In this context, see Galit Hasan-Rokem, "The Snake at the Wedding: Semiotic Reconsideration of the Comparative Method of Folk Narrative Research" (in Hebrew), *Criticism and Interpretation: Journal for Literature, Linguistics, History and Aesthetics* 30 (1994), 36.
20. Ruhama Weiss, *Meal Tests: The Meal in the World of the Sages* (in Hebrew) (Bnei Brak: Hakibbutz Hameuchad, 2010), 211–217.
21. Note that in several manuscripts (MS Munich 95 and MS Oxford), the Aramaic verb for her giving to the beggar appears in plural form, slightly blurring the specific father-daughter drama between R. Akiva and his daughter, although the daughter's act of choice is still preserved. The portion she had been given by the banquet's participants she chooses to give to a specific man, an outsider, whose voice only she hears and whom, to some extent, she chooses.
22. See Sigmund Freud, *The Uncanny*, trans. David Mclintock (London: Penguin Books, 2003), 139, for his well-known reference to this issue: "The study of dreams, fantasies and myths has taught us also that anxiety about one's eyes, the fear of going blind, is quite often a substitute for the fear of castration. When the mythical criminal Oedipus blinds himself, this is merely a mitigated form of the penalty of castration."

23. For further discussion of the story, see Fraenkel, *Studies*, 13–16; Ari Elon, "The Symbolization of the Plot Elements in the Talmudic Story" (in Hebrew) (master's thesis, Hebrew University of Jerusalem, 1982), 67–70. On the folk characteristics of the story, see Hasan-Rokem, "The Snake at the Wedding," 35–36.
24. The phrase "Ewe follows ewe" is defined by the narrator as a proverb and therefore works as such in this story. In some of the manuscripts, as noted, this proverb is missing, and the proverb the text refers to is "like mother, like daughter" (MS Munich 95). For comprehensive research reviews about the definition of the proverb and its cultural and political contexts, see, for example, Peter Seitel, "Proverbs: A Social Use of Metaphor," *Genre* 2 (1969): 143–161; Galit Hasan-Rokem, *Proverbs in Israeli Folk Narrative: A Structural Semantic Analysis* (Folklore Fellows Communications, 232) (Helsinki: Suomalainen Tiedeakatemia, Academia Scientiarum Fennica, 1982); Wolfgang Mieder, *Proverbs Are Never Out of Season: Popular Wisdom in the Modern Age* (New York: Oxford University Press, 1993); Haim Weiss, "Did the Straw Indeed Break the Camel's Back? Three Theoretical Aspects in the Study of Proverbs" (in Hebrew), *Jerusalem Studies in Jewish Folklore* 21 (2001): 163–182; Tamar Alexander, *Words Are Better Than Bread: A Study of the Judeo-Spanish Proverb* (in Hebrew) (Jerusalem: Ben Zvi Institute, 2004); Galit Hasan-Rokem, "Negotiating Canons: Rabbinic Proverbs Between Oral Tradition and Scripture," in *Bis dat, Qui cito dat: Gegengabe in Paremiology, Folklore, and Literature Honoring Wolfgang Mieder on His Seventieth Birthday*, ed. Christian Grandl and Kevin J. McKenna (Frankfurt am Main: Peter Lang, 2015), 163–179.
25. Hasan-Rokem, *Proverbs in Israeli Folk Narrative*, 12, summing up Petsch's view. For a citation of Petsch, see Hasan-Rokem, "The Proverb as Interpretation: The Interpretation of a Proverb" (in Hebrew), *Yeda 'Am* 45–46 (1979): 74.
26. In this context, see Boyarin's comment on the meaning of the story's ending: "The story encodes the extreme model of Rachel as an ideal for Jewish womanhood and not as an exception" (Boyarin, *Carnal Israel*, 154).
27. On this issue, see also Ilan, *Mine and Yours Are Hers*, 120.

28. For a parallel version, see Genesis Rabba 34; BT Yevamot 63b. In the Babylonian Talmud (Sotah 4b), Ben Azzai is even described as one who never married. The tosafists address the contradiction between the two sources and suggest an interesting solution: "and although it says here that she did so to Ben Azzai, he did not marry her and they were only engaged" (Tosafot on BT Ketubot 63a). The tosafists' solution creates a complete analogy between the mother's and the daughter's deeds. Just as the Ketubot story describes a situation wherein Ben Kalba Savu'a's daughter was only engaged to R. Akiva, so too does the daughter create a liminal couplehood with Ben Azzai whereby they are simultaneously married and not married. The definition of their couplehood as an engagement enables dismissal of the contradiction between the texts in Ketubot and in Sotah while emphasizing the power of the daughter's imitative move.
29. Even the reference to the many presents of silver and gold with which R. Akiva showered his wife (see note 11 above) entails an exaggeration far beyond good taste, at least in the perception of his disciples.

THE SEVENTH STORY

1. For a reading of this story, see Shmuel Faust, *Agadata: Stories of Talmudic Drama* (in Hebrew) (Or Yehuda: Kinneret/Zmora Bitan/Dvir, 2011), 160–164.
2. Ibid., 161–163.
3. The association between the dove and women/womanhood is known and widespread in all branches of ancient literature: The literature of the ancient Near East, biblical literature, Midrash literature, Greco-Roman literature, and early Christian literature all include various expressions of these associations. In rabbinic literature, and in Christian literature as well, the sexual and erotic images of the dove originate in the Song of Songs, where the lover describes his beloved as a dove: "you are beautiful, my love; you are beautiful; your eyes are doves" (Song of Songs 1:15). These descriptions undergo allegorical transformation and are made to represent the people of Israel or the Church. The female qualities expressed in the dove's character are modesty,

obedience, and loyalty, with the woman surrendering to the will of God or her husband. For an extensive discussion of the dove's image in Jewish and Christian traditions, see Irit Ziffer, *O My Dove, That Art in the Clefts of the Rock: The Dove Allegory in Antiquity* (exhibition Catalogue), trans. Joseph Shadur and Irit Ziffer (Tel Aviv: Tel Aviv Museum, 1998), 95–113.

4. Yona Fraenkel, *Studies on the Spiritual World of the Aggadic Story* (in Hebrew) (Tel Aviv: Hakibbutz Hameuchad, 1981), 112–115.
5. Daniel Boyarin, *Carnal Israel: Reading Sex in Talmudic Culture* (Berkeley: University of California Press, 1993), 155.
6. Shulamit Valler, who devotes a very brief analysis (one short paragraph) to the last story, also claims that the purpose of the story is to emphasize "how very serious the conflict was." See Shulamit Valler, *Women and Womanhood in the Talmud*, trans. Betty Sigler Rozen (Providence, RI: Brown University, 1999), 74.

EPILOGUE

1. The story, in the translation of David S. Segal, is included in *A Book That Was Lost: And Other Stories by S. Y. Agnon*, ed. Alan Mintz and Anne Golomb Hoffman (New York: Schocken Books, 1995). Subsequent page references to this work will be cited parenthetically in the text. Another version of this story, shorter and earlier, titled "Between the House and the Yard" (*Bein ha-bayit la-hatser*), appeared in the collection *Sefer ha-Mo 'adim* (collected by Y. L. Baruch), in 1946.
2. Haim Be'er directed our attention to a biographical testimony that might be related to the story we are discussing. It appears in the autobiographical book of Emunah Yaron, Agnon's daughter, in two versions. One reads: "One Shabbat eve we sat at one of the synagogues, but the prayer leader did not begin prayers. The congregation, which lost patience, called *Nu*! *Nu*! to which the leader replied, 'In a place where there is a female, I cannot pray.' Father got up, took his female, who was about five, and announced, 'In a place where the prayer leader harbors such thoughts, I cannot pray,' and we walked out" (Emunah Yaron, *Chapters from My Life* (in Hebrew) [Jerusalem, Schocken, 2005], 75.)

The other version reads: "I was small and could go with father to all the synagogues. It only happened once that the prayer leader interrupted his prayers, covered his face with his *tallit*, and proclaimed, 'A female is here! I will not pray until you take the female out of the synagogue.' Father got up, took my hand, and said, 'I will not pray with a leader who harbors strange thoughts in his heart.' And we went out. I was not yet five" (ibid., 248). This testimony is particularly interesting, given the father's yearning in Agnon's story: "Would that they might appoint a reader of prayers worthy to stand before the ark, for recent generations have seen the decline of emissaries of the congregation who know how to pray. . . . And I, I need strengthening—and needless to say, my little daughter, a babe torn away from her home" (371). The testimony emphasizes Agnon's strong stance vis-à-vis the prayer leader in contrast with the failed father in the story, who does not protest the mocking of the congregation members who ban him and his naked daughter. His daughter is the one who asks to leave the synagogue immediately, but he resists, and insists on remaining in the place where they had been humiliated.

3. See Baruch Kurzweil, *Essays on S. Y. Agnon's Stories* (in Hebrew) (Jerusalem: Schocken, 1964), 175–187; Yaakov Bahat, "'At the Outset of the Day' by S. Y. Agnon: Sources and Review" (in Hebrew), *Ha-Hinukh* 39, nos. 1–6 (1967): 121–127; Samuel Leiter, ed., *Selected Stories of S. Y. Agnon* (New York: Tarbut Foundation, 1970); Edna Aphek, *Word Systems: Readings in the Style of S. Y. Agnon* (in Hebrew) (Tel Aviv: Dekel, 1979); Rachel Ofer, "'At the Outset of the Day': Days of Awe and Repentance in S. Y. Agnon's *Oeuvre*" (in Hebrew), in *Repentance and Psychology*, ed. Hayyim Navon (Alon Shevut: Tevunot, 2011), 67–76.
4. "The narrator explicitly provides us here with the key: The girl is the soul that disguised itself as a girl, not in order to show its purity but to hint at its yearnings." Ofer, "Days of Awe and Repentance," 74.
5. Kurzweil, *Essays*, 176.
6. As in the story of R. Akiva and Rachel discussed earlier, here, too, the pure and mortified female body, lacking any cover or adornment, yields knowledge and wisdom in a primary, almost natural mode that precedes the male modes of study and memorizing taking place at the *beth*

midrash: The young daughter, whose shirt burns in the fire, remains naked in the synagogue, and only her hair covers her body. Nevertheless, her prayer melodies, mumbled in her sleep, are described as "sweet melodies no ear has ever heard" (377). According to a similar principle, R. Akiva's wife refuses to wear smarter clothes when going to meet her husband, who is returning after an absence of twenty-four years. The dialogue between her and her neighbors creates a reverse link between clothing and intuitive knowledge ("a righteous man knows the soul of his beast").

7. Yom Kippur, with the theological tension it embodies between sin and atonement and between body and soul, occupied Agnon in several stories. For a partial anthology of Agnon's stories on Yom Kippur, see Naphtali Ginaton, *Stories on Yom Kippur* (in Hebrew) (Jerusalem: Schocken, 1967). On the meaning of the Yom Kippur stories in Agnon's work, see Kurzweil, *Essays*, 269–282; Malka Shaked, "The Problem of Yom Kippur and Its Solution in Agnon's *Oeuvre*" (in Hebrew), in *Studies on Agnon*, ed. Hillel Weiss and Hillel Barzel (Ramat-Gan: Bar-Ilan University Press, 1994). Besides the tension between holiness and sin, and due to it, Yom Kippur is also a familiar backdrop in nineteenth- and early twentieth-century Hebrew literature that addresses the split between members of the new and old generations in the Jewish community. Against the background of the day's holiness, the tensions between fathers and sons intensify, as in the stories *Le'an?* (Where To?) by Mordecai Zeev Feierberg (1899); *Me-ever la-Nahar* (Beyond the River) by Micha Yosef Berdyczewski (1899), and *Se 'udah Mefaseket* (The Meal Before the Fast) by Uri Nissan Gnessin (1905). In *Yom ha-Din shel Faivke* (Faivke's Doomsday) by Y. D. Berkowitz (1912), for example, the tension turns into a horrid confrontation between barbarity and culture, between routine observance and holiness, between Jews and Gentiles, between parents and their child, and between good and evil—a confrontation that is tragically resolved through violence and the child's death.

8. *Sifre: A Tannaitic Commentary on the Book of Deuteronomy*, trans. Reuven Hammer (New Haven, CT: Yale University Press, 1986), Piska 305, 295. For parallel versions, see also *The Fathers According to Rabbi*

Nathan, trans. Judah Goldin (New Haven, CT: Yale University Press, 1955), version A, ch. 17; BT Ketubot 66b–67a. For a partial parallel version, see Lamentations Rabba (Buber) 1.

9. On Agnon and Song of Songs, see Ilana Pardes, *Agnon's Moonstruck Lovers: The Song of Songs in Israeli Culture* (Seattle: University of Washington Press, 2013).

BIBLIOGRAPHY

Abarbanell, Nitza. *Eve and Lilith* (in Hebrew). Ramat-Gan: Bar-Ilan University Press, 1994.

Agnon, S. Y. "At the Outset of the Day." Trans. David S. Segal. In *A Book That Was Lost: And Other Stories*, ed. Alan Mintz and Anne Golomb Hoffman, 370–377. New York: Schocken Books, 1995.

Alexander, Tamar. *Words Are Better Than Bread: A Study of the Judeo-Spanish Proverb* (in Hebrew). Jerusalem: Ben Zvi Institute, 2004.

Alon, Gedalyahu. "The Sociological Method in the Study of Halakhah" (in Hebrew). In *Studies in Jewish History in the Times of the Second Temple, the Mishnah and the Talmud*, vol. 2, 181–227. Tel Aviv: Hakibbutz Hameuchad, 1978.

Alter, Robert. *The Art of Biblical Narrative.* New York: Basic Books, 1981.

Aphek, Edna. *Word Systems: Readings in the Style of S. Y. Agnon* (in Hebrew). Tel Aviv: Dekel, 1979.

Bahat, Yaakov. "'At the Outset of the Day' by S. Y. Agnon: Sources and Review" (in Hebrew). *Ha-Khinukh* 39, nos. 1–6 (1967): 121–127.

Baker, Cynthia. *Rebuilding the House of Israel: Architectures of Gender in Jewish Antiquity.* Stanford, CA: Stanford University Press, 2002.

Balberg, Mira. "Between Heterotopias and Utopias: Two Rabbinic Stories about Journeys to Prostitutes" (in Hebrew). *Jerusalem Studies in Hebrew Literature* 22 (2008): 191–213.

Bar-Asher Siegal, Michal. *Early Christian Monastic Literature and the Babylonian Talmud*. New York: Cambridge University Press, 2013.

Baskin, Judith R. *Midrashic Women: Formations of the Feminine in Rabbinic Literature*. Hanover, NH: Brandeis University Press, 2002.

Ben-Pazzi, Yeshayahu. "The Biblical and Midrashic Context as a Tool in the Understanding of Rabbinic Aggadot" (in Hebrew). *Hemdat* 6 (2009): 47–71.

Boose, Lynda E. "The Father's House and the Daughter in It." In *Daughters and Fathers*, ed. Lynda E. Boose and Betty S. Flowers, 19–74. Baltimore, MD: Johns Hopkins University Press, 1989.

Bourdieu, Pierre. *Masculine Domination*. Trans. Richard Nice. Stanford, CA: Stanford University Press, 2002.

Boyarin, Daniel. *Carnal Israel: Reading Sex in Talmudic Culture*. Berkeley: University of California Press, 1993.

Bronner, Leila Leah. *From Eve to Esther: Rabbinic Reconstructions of Biblical Women*. Louisville, KY: Westminster John Knox Press, 1994.

Calderon, Ruth. *A Bride for One Night: Talmud Tales*. Trans. Ilana Kurshan. Lincoln /Philadelphia: University of Nebraska Press/Jewish Publication Society, 2014.

Chodorow Nancy. *The Reproduction of Mothering: Psychoanalysis and the Sociology of Gender*. Berkeley: University of California Press, 1979.

Collins Bursi, Adam. "Holy Spit and Magic Spells: Religion, Magic and the Body in Late Ancient Judaism, Christianity, and Islam." PhD diss., Cornell University, 2015.

Elbaum, Jacob. "Models of Storytelling and Speech in Stories about the Sages" (in Hebrew). *Proceedings of the Seventh World Congress of Jewish Studies* 7 (1977): 71–77.

Elon, Ari. "The Symbolization of the Plot Elements in the Talmudic Story" (in Hebrew). Master's thesis, Hebrew University of Jerusalem, 1982.

———. *Alma Di* (in Hebrew). Tel Aviv: Miskal, 2011.

Euripides, *Alcestis*. Trans. David Kovacs. Cambridge, MA: Harvard University Press, 1994.

Eydar, Dror. "The Art of the Jewish-Persian Tale in the Middle Ages: A Study of the Story of R. Akiva and His Wife in Fourteenth- and Sixteenth-Century Manuscripts" (in Hebrew). *Jewish Studies, an Internet Journal* 9 (2010).

Ezrahi, Ohad, and Mordechai Gafni. *Who's Afraid of Lilith: Re-reading the Kabbalah of the Feminine Shadow* (in Hebrew). Ben-Shemen: Modan, 2005.

The Fathers According to Rabbi Nathan. Trans. Judah Goldin. New Haven, CT: Yale University Press, 1955.

Faust, Shmuel. "Criticism in Sages' Stories from the Babylonian Talmud." PhD diss., Bar-Ilan University, 2010.

———. *Agadata: Stories of Talmudic Drama* (in Hebrew). Or Yehuda: Kinneret/Zmora Bitan/Dvir, 2011.

Fisher, Esther. "'His *Yetzer* Is External, Her *Yetzer* Is Internal': Gendered Aspects of Sexual Desire in Rabbinic Literature" (in Hebrew). PhD diss., Bar-Ilan University, 2014.

Fonrobert, Charlotte Elisheva. *Menstrual Purity: Rabbinic and Christian Reconstructions of Biblical Gender*. Stanford, CA: Stanford University Press, 2000.

———. "When the Rabbi Weeps: On Reading Gender in Talmudic Aggadah." *Nashim: A Journal of Jewish Women's Studies & Gender Issues* 4 (2001): 56–83.

Fraenkel, Yona. "Hermeneutic Problems in the Study of the Aggadic Narrative" (in Hebrew). *Tarbiz* 47 (1978): 107–256.

———. *Studies on the Spiritual World of the Aggadic Story* (in Hebrew). Tel Aviv: Hakibbutz Hameuchad, 1981.

———. *On Aggadah and Midrash* (in Hebrew). Ramat-Gan: Yad la-Talmud, 1991.

Freud, Sigmund. *Moses and Monotheism*. Trans. Katherine Jones. London: Hogarth Press/Institute of Psychoanalysis, 1939.

———. *On Sexuality: Three Essays on the Theory of Sexuality*. Trans. James Strachey. London: Penguin Books, 1991.

———. *The Uncanny*. Trans. David McLintock. London: Penguin Books, 2003.

Friedman, Shamma. "A Good Story Deserves Retelling: The Unfolding of the Akiva Legend." In *Creation and Composition: The Contribution of the Bavli Redactors (Stammaim) to the Aggadah*, ed. Jeffrey L. Rubenstein, 71–100. Tübingen: Mohr-Siebeck, 2005.

Gallop, Jane. *The Daughter's Seduction: Feminism and Psychoanalysis.* Ithaca, NY: Cornell University Press, 1982.

Ginaton, Naphtali. *Stories on Yom Kippur* (in Hebrew). Jerusalem: Schocken, 1967.

Girard, René. *Deceit, Desire, and the Novel: Self and Other in Literary Structure*. Trans. Yvonne Freccero. Baltimore, MD: Johns Hopkins University Press, 1972.

Godelier, Maurice. "The Origins of Male Domination." *New Left Review* 127 (May–June 1981): 3–17.

Hartmann, Heidi. "The Unhappy Marriage of Marxism and Feminism: Towards a More Progressive Union." In *Feminist Theory Reader: Local and Global Perspectives*, ed. Carole McCann and Seung-Kyung Kim, 206–221. New York: Routledge, 2017.

Hasan-Rokem, Galit. "The Proverb as Interpretation: The Interpretation of a Proverb" (in Hebrew). *Yeda 'Am* 45–46 (1979): 74–78.

———. "The Biblical Verse as Proverb and as Quote" (in Hebrew). *Jerusalem Studies in Hebrew Literature* 1 (1981): 155–166.

———. *Proverbs in Israeli Folk Narrative: A Structural Semantic Analysis* (Folklore Fellows Communications, 232). Helsinki: Suomalainen Tiedeakatemia, Academia Scientiarum Fennica, 1982.

———. "The Snake at the Wedding: Semiotic Reconsideration of the Comparative Method of Folk Narrative Research" (in Hebrew). *Criticism and Interpretation: Journal for Literature, Linguistics, History and Aesthetics* 30 (1994): 26–40.

———. "The Three-Folded Cord: On Sexuality, Couplehood, and Womanhood in Rabbinic Literature" (in Hebrew). *Theory and Criticism* 7 (1995): 255–264.

———. *Web of Life: Folklore and Midrash in Rabbinic Literature.* Trans. Batya Stein. Stanford, CA: Stanford University Press, 2000.

———. *Tales of the Neighborhood: Jewish Narrative Dialogues in Late Antiquity*. Berkeley: University of California Press, 2003.

———. "Negotiating Canons: Rabbinic Proverbs between Oral Tradition and Scripture." In *Bis dat, Qui cito dat: Gegengabe in Paremiology, Folklore, and Literature Honoring Wolfgang Mieder on His Seventieth Birthday*, ed. Christian Grandl and Kevin J. McKenna, 163–179. Frankfurt am Main: Peter Lang, 2015.

Ilan, Tal. *Mine and Yours Are Hers: Retrieving Women's History from Rabbinic Literature.* Leiden: Brill, 1997.

———. "The Daughters of Zelophehad and Women's Inheritance: The Biblical Injunction and Its Outcome." In *A Feminist Companion to the Bible: Exodus to Deuteronomy* (second series), ed. Athalya Brenner, 176–186. Sheffield: Sheffield Academic Press, 2000.

———. "'Jerusalem of Gold' and the Historical Kernel in the Stories of R. Akiva's Wife" (in Hebrew). In *A Woman in Jerusalem: Gender, Society, and Religion*, ed. Tova Cohen and Joshua Schwartz, 33–46. Ramat-Gan: Bar Ilan University, 2002.

Irigaray, Luce. *This Sex Which Is Not One.* Trans. Catherine Porter. Ithaca, NY: Cornell University Press, 1985.

Israeli, Oded. "*Kiddushin*, Marriage, and Torah Study in the Stories of R. Akiva and the Daughter of Kalba Savu'a" (in Hebrew). *Assufot: Journal on Aggadah and Midrash* 1 (2010–2011): 94–104.

Kalmin, Richard. *The Sage in Jewish Society of Late Antiquity.* London: Routledge, 1999.

Kara-Ivanov Kaniel, Ruth. *Holiness and Transgression: Mothers of the Messiah in the Jewish Myth.* Trans. Eugene D. Matanky with Ruth Kara-Ivanov Kaniel. Boston: Academic Studies Press, 2017.

Katz, Menachem, and Israel Rosensohn. "'Fig, Bring Forth Your Fruit': The Stories of R. Jose of Yokeret" (in Hebrew). *Derekh Aggadah* 3 (2000): 161–177.

Kosman, Admiel. *Women's Tractate: Wisdom, Love, Faithfulness, Passion, Beauty, Sex, Holiness* (in Hebrew). Jerusalem: Keter, 2007.

———. *Men's World: Reading Masculinity in Jewish Stories in a Spiritual Context.* Trans. Edward Levin. Würzburg: Ergon, 2009.

Kosofsky Sedgwick, Eve. *Between Men: English Literature and Male Homosocial Desire.* New York: Columbia University Press, 1985.

Kristeva, Julia. "Women's Time." Trans. Alice Jardine and Harry Blake. *Signs* 7, no. 1 (1981): 13–35.

Kurzweil, Baruch. *Essays on S. Y. Agnon's Stories* (in Hebrew). Jerusalem: Schocken, 1964.

Lacan, Jacques. *Écrits: A Selection*. Trans. Alan Sheridan. London: Tavistock, 1977.

Lavee, Moshe. "Acceptance of Other and Otherness: Processes of Emphasis and Ambiguity in Rabbinic Narratives" (in Hebrew). *Mishlav* 37 (2001):75–114.

Leiter, Samuel, ed., *Selected Stories of S. Y. Agnon*. New York: Tarbut Foundation, 1970.

Levinson, Joshua. *The Twice-Told Tale: A Poetics of the Exegetical Narrative in Rabbinic Midrash* (in Hebrew). Jerusalem: Magnes, 2005.

———. "From Parable to Invention: The Growth of Fiction as a Cultural Category" (in Hebrew). In *Higayon l'Yona: New Aspects in the Study of Midrash, Aggadah, and Piyut in Honor of Professor Yona Fraenkel*, ed. Joshua Levinson, Jacob Elbaum, and Galit Hasan-Rokem, 1–32. Jerusalem: Magnes Press, 2006.

Lévi-Strauss, Claude. *The Elementary Structures of Kinship*. Trans. James Harle Bell. Boston: Beacon Press, 1969.

Madar, Vered. "Yemenite Women's Songs for the Parturient and Their Laments over the Dead: Text, Body, and Voice" (in Hebrew). PhD diss., Hebrew University of Jerusalem, 2011.

Marienberg-Milikowsky, Itay. "'Beyond the Matter': Stories and Their Contexts in the Babylonian Talmud—Repeated Stories as a Test Case" (in Hebrew). PhD diss., Ben-Gurion University of the Negev, 2015.

Marks, Susan. "Follow That Crown: Or, Rhetoric, Rabbis, and Women Patrons." *Journal of Feminist Studies in Religion* 24 (2008): 77–96.

Meir, Ofra. *R. Judah the Patriarch: Palestinian and Babylonian Portrait of a Leader* (in Hebrew). Tel Aviv: Hakibbutz Hameuchad, 1999.

Mieder, Wolfgang. *Proverbs Are Never Out of Season: Popular Wisdom in the Modern Age*. New York: Oxford University Press, 1993.

Miller, David Lee. "The Body of Fatherhood." *ANQ: A Quarterly Journal of Short Articles, Notes and Reviews* 15 (2002): 3–16.

Myerowitz Levine, Molly. "Women Who Wait: Akiva's Rahel and Odysseus' Penelope." In *Hellenic and Jewish Arts: Interaction, Tradition and Renewal*, ed. Asher Ovadiah, 303–335. Tel Aviv: Ramot, 1998.

Neis, Rachael. *The Sense of Sight in Rabbinic Culture: Jewish Ways of Seeing in Late Antiquity*. Cambridge University Press, 2013.

Ofer, Rachel. "'At the Outset of the Day': Days of Awe and Repentance in S. Y. Agnon's *Oeuvre*" (in Hebrew). In *Repentance and Psychology*, ed. Hayyim Navon, 67–76. Alon Shevut: Tevunot, 2011.

Oppenheimer, Aharon. *Rabbi Judah ha-Nasi* (in Hebrew). Jerusalem: Zalman Shazar Center for Jewish History, 2007.

Ortner, Sherry B. "Is Female to Male as Nature Is to Culture?" In *Women, Culture, and Society*, ed. Michelle Zimbalist Rosaldo, Louise Lamphere, and Joan Bamberger, 68–87. Stanford, CA: Stanford University Press, 1974.

Owen, Ursula. *Fathers: Reflections by Daughters.* New York: Pantheon Books, 1985.

Pardes, Ilana. *Agnon's Moonstruck Lovers: The Song of Songs in Israeli Culture.* Seattle: University of Washington Press, 2013.

Rank, Otto. *The Incest Theme in Literature and Legend: Fundamentals of a Psychology of Literary Creation*. Trans. Gregory C. Richter. Baltimore, MD: Johns Hopkins University Press, 1992.

Rose, Jacqueline. "Introduction—II," to Jacques Lacan, *Feminine Sexuality: Jacques Lacan and the École Freudienne.* Trans. Jacqueline Rose. New York: Pantheon Books, 1985.

Rubenstein, Jeffrey. *Rabbinic Stories.* New York: Paulist Press, 2002.

———. *The Culture of the Babylonian Talmud.* Baltimore, MD: Johns Hopkins University Press, 2003.

Rubin, Gayle. "The Traffic in Women: Notes on the 'Political Economy' of Sex." In *Toward an Anthropology of Women*, ed. Rayna Reiter, 157–210. New York: Monthly Review Press, 1975.

Rubin, Nissan. *The End of Life: Rites of Burial and Mourning in the Talmud and Midrash* (in Hebrew). Tel Aviv: Hakibbutz Hameuchad, 1997.

———. *The Joy of Life: Rites of Betrothal and Marriage in the Talmud and Midrash* (in Hebrew). Tel Aviv: Hakibbutz Hameuchad, 2004.

Safrai, Shmuel. *R. Akiva ben Yosef: His Life and Teachings* (in Hebrew). Jerusalem: Bialik Institute, 1978.

Satlow, Michael L. *Jewish Marriage in Antiquity*. Princeton, NJ: Princeton University Press, 2001.

Schremer, Adiel. *Male and Female He Created Them: Jewish Marriage in the Late Second Temple, Mishnah, and Talmud Periods* (in Hebrew). Jerusalem: Zalman Shazar Center for Jewish History, 2003.

Scott, Joan W. "Gender: A Useful Category of Historical Analysis." *American Historical Review* 91 (1986): 1053–1075.

Sebba-Elran, Tsafi. "R. Yossi of Yokeret and the Modern Jewish Anthologies" (in Hebrew). In *Folklore and Ideology: Studies Dedicated to Prof. Aliza Shenhar*, edi. Haya Bar-Itzhak, 133–163. Haifa: Pardes, 2014.

Seitel, Peter. "Proverbs: A Social Use of Metaphor." *Genre* 2 (1969): 143–161.

Shabtai, Aharon. Introduction to the Hebrew translation of *Alcestis*, by Euripides. Jerusalem: Schocken, 1986.

Shaked, Malka. "The Problem of Yom Kippur and Its Solution in Agnon's *Oeuvre*" (in Hebrew). In *Studies on Agnon* (in Hebrew), ed. Hillel Weiss and Hillel Barzel, 321–335. Ramat-Gan: Bar-Ilan University Press, 1994.

Shinan, Avigdor. "The Three Wives of R. Akiva" (in Hebrew). *Masekhet* 2 (2004): 11–25.

Shoshany, Ronit. "The Story of the Carpenter's Apprentice" (in Hebrew). *Sidra: A Journal for the Study of Rabbinic Literature* 21 (2006): 87–98.

Spillers, Hortense. "'The Permanent Obliquity of an In[pha]llibly Straight': In the Times of the Daughters and Fathers." In *Daughters and Fathers*, ed. Lynda E. Boose and Betty S. Flowers, 157–176. Baltimore, MD: Johns Hopkins University Press, 1989.

Stav, Shira. *Reconstructing Daddy: Fathers and Daughters in Modern Hebrew Poetry* (in Hebrew). Or Yehuda/Beer Sheva: Dvir/Ben-Gurion University of the Negev, 2014.

Stein, Dina. *Maxims, Magic, Myth: A Folkloristic Perspective of Pirkei deRabbi Eliezer* (in Hebrew). Jerusalem: Magnes Press, 2004.

———. "Collapsing Structures: Discourse and the Destruction of the Temple in the Babylonian Talmud." *Jewish Quarterly Review* 98, no. 1 (2008): 1–28.

———. "Identity, Absence, and Return: Reading Two Rabbinic Stories." (in Hebrew). In *Childhood Memory and Forgetfulness: Revisiting Odysseus' Scar*, ed. Vered Lev Kenaan and Noga Weiss, 189–201. Haifa: Haifa University Press, 2018.

Valler, Shulamit. *Women and Womanhood in the Talmud.* Trans. Betty Sigler Rozen. Providence, RI: Brown University, 1999.

———. "Domestic Strife and Domestic Harmony in the Literature of the Sages" (in Hebrew). In *Peace and War in Jewish Culture*, ed. Avriel Bar-Levav, 11–33. Jerusalem: Zalman Shazar Center for Jewish History, 2006.

———. *Sorrow and Distress in the Talmud.* Trans. Sharon Blass. Boston: Academic Studies Press, 2011.

Walden, Noa. "Weeping in Rabbinic Literature: Cultural, Literary, and Rhetorical Aspects" (in Hebrew). Master's thesis, Ben-Gurion University of the Negev, 2012.

Weiss, Haim. "Did the Straw Indeed Break the Camel's Back? Three Theoretical Aspects in the Study of Proverbs" (in Hebrew). *Jerusalem Studies in Jewish Folklore* 21 (2001): 163–182.

———. "Worthless Son of Worthy Father? Political Struggles, Torah Study, and Identity in the Family of R. Shimon Bar Yohai" (in Hebrew). In *Peace and War in Jewish Culture*, ed. Avriel Bar-Levav, 67–83. Jerusalem: Zalman Shazar Center for Jewish History, 2006.

———. *All Dreams Follow the Mouth: A Reading in the Talmudic Dreams Tractate* (in Hebrew). Or Yehuda: Dvir, 2011.

Weiss, Ruhama. *Meal Tests: The Meal in the World of the Sages* (in Hebrew). Bnei Brak: Hakibbutz Hameuchad, 2010.

Yaron, Emunah. *Chapters from My Life* (in Hebrew). Jerusalem: Schocken, 2005.

Yassif, Eli. "The Cycle of Tales in Rabbinic Literature" (in Hebrew). *Jerusalem Studies in Hebrew Literature* 12 (1990): 103–145.

Ziffer, Irit. *O My Dove, That Art in the Clefts of the Rock: The Dove Allegory in Antiquity* (exhibition catalogue). Trans. Joseph Shadur and Irit Ziffer, 95–113. Tel Aviv: Tel Aviv Museum, 1998.

Zimmer, Yitzhak. "Lowering the Bed in Mourning" (in Hebrew). *Sinai* 115 (1995): 228–252.

Zimmerman, David. *Eight Love Stories from Talmud and Midrash* (in Hebrew). Tel Aviv: Sifriat Poalim, 1981.

Žižek, Slavoj. *Looking Awry: An Introduction to Jacques Lacan Through Popular Culture.* Cambridge, MA: MIT Press, 1993.

SOURCE INDEX

NAME INDEX

SUBJECT INDEX

CPSIA information can be obtained
at www.ICGtesting.com
Printed in the USA
JSHW050809261221
21519JS00001B/2

9 780812 253634